IN DEFENSE
OF CHARISMA

IN DEFENSE
OF CHARISMA

VINCENT W. LLOYD

Columbia University Press   *New York*

Columbia University Press
Publishers Since 1893
New York   Chichester, West Sussex
cup.columbia.edu

Cataloging-in-Publication Data available from the
Library of Congress.
Names: Lloyd, Vincent W., 1982– author.
Title: In defense of charisma / Vincent W. Lloyd.
Description: New York : Columbia University Press, [2018] |
Includes bibliographical references and index.
Identifiers: LCCN 2017039169 | ISBN 9780231183864
(cloth: acid-free paper) | ISBN 9780231183871 (pbk.) |
ISBN 9780231545204 (e-book)
Subjects: LCSH: Charisma (Personality trait) | Authority.
Classification: LCC BF698.35.C45 L55 2018 | DDC 155.2/32—dc23
LC record available at https://lccn.loc.gov/2017039169

Cover design: Jordan Wannemacher

For my daughter

CONTENTS

IN DEFENSE
OF CHARISMA

INTRODUCTION

Charisma has fallen into disrepute. Scholars are suspicious of it. When the word is used in politics, it brings with it ambivalence, the sense that charisma might be a necessary evil. Celebrities may be charismatic, but such charisma has little more than entertainment value. Books about charisma are now found in the business and self-help sections of bookstores. Handbooks, websites, and workshops offer to teach charisma in order to make you a better boss, to make you a future executive, or to help you make friends. Everyone cannot become a movie star, but anyone can become more charismatic—just follow these ten steps. Understood in this way, charisma appears democratic. Charisma is not a gift bestowed upon a few; it is a skill open to all who are willing to put in the work, to follow the steps. But the charisma of the corporate executive, or of the manager of a fast food franchise, seems distant from the conceptual core of charisma. Whether our paradigm is Hitler or Churchill, Gandhi or King, Audrey Hepburn or Cary Grant, charisma connotes a certain nobility or greatness at odds with the world of the hamburger flipper and at odds with the world of the middle manager.

Perhaps it is not nobility that is lost in the way we talk about charisma today but rather the normative, the sense that charisma can be good or bad, that charisma can advance justice or mask injustice. Whether it is applied to the entertainer or to the business leader, charisma is pragmatic. It is useful in accomplishing a goal: providing entertainment or building a business. If charisma is said to be good, its goodness is instrumental. It is good insofar as it assists an entertainer or business manager in becoming a better entertainer or business manager. Philip Rieff aptly labels this "spray-on charisma," characteristic of our modern, secular age. In collective, public endeavors today we are concerned with what works. Questions about what is true, what is good, and what is beautiful—without qualification, without limit to a particular context or goal—are questions to contemplate in private, to decide for oneself, if they are worth addressing at all. The normative dimension of charisma is necessarily foreclosed. If charisma is, by definition, public, we must turn away from charisma when we contemplate the most serious questions. Charisma may have once had normative significance, perhaps in the days of Moses or St. Francis, but such significance is gone in our modern world, replaced by the instrumental.

Such a separation between public and private is, of course, a convenient fiction constructed by the theorist of modernity, and it has little relevance to how modernity is lived. Scholars of religion have thought carefully about the porous boundaries between public and private, the artificial construction of this distinction, and the way that religious ideas, practices, and beliefs circulate widely even when they are felt individually. While once modernity was thought to precipitate secularity, with religion relegated to the heart of the individual believer, where it would gradually fade away, the continuing significance of religious communities and of barely secularized religious ideas in the public sphere is a powerful reminder that our modern world is not as straightforwardly secular as its theorists would make it out to be. When stories are told about the postsecular, as the academic trend for questioning the traditional connection between modernity and secularity has come to be known, they are usually stories that straddle the supposed divide between the religious and the secular. Yet much of the significance of the postsecular is lost when it simply comes to mean finding religion in new, unexpected places (in sporting events, or political speeches, or consumer culture). The most profound implication of the postsecular is to open up normative questions—for religion is, after all, unthinkable without normativity. Religious traditions debate what is good, and true, and beautiful. When it becomes clear that religion can no longer be relegated to the heart, that religion and culture (including the very act of scholarship or theorizing itself) are inextricably linked, it means that those of us who are interested in reflecting on contemporary culture must also be thinking about those normative questions. If we bracket what is good, what is true, and what is beautiful in the pursuit of value-free description, we are effectively acceding to the picture of private and public domains painted by modernity—which has been given the lie. In short, there is a new conversation about charisma that we ought to be having. It is not about whether charisma is useful but rather about how charisma opens a normative world, allowing us to see what ought to be the case—and motivating us to make the world more just.

When scholars study charisma today, they approach the topic with suspicion. While a wave of political leaders a generation ago was described in the media as charismatic—Castro, Sukarno, Nkrumah, to name but three—and this prompted political scientists and sociologists to probe whether charisma is an analytically useful concept, more recent scholars have concerned themselves with revealing what charisma conceals. Whether the charismatic figure is advancing bad politics (Hitler) or good (King), or just entertaining (Beyoncé), charisma enchants. That such enchantment is considered a problem can be read as a symptom of our secular age. But it also suggests that scholars of this persuasion, which is to say, most scholars who write about charisma, do in fact have normative commitments that they advance through their study of charisma. It is the normative commitment of the secularist: religion is inherently deceitful, unsightly, and morally suspect, and so is charisma. Religion, or charisma, might have influence in our contemporary world, and it might be important to track and unpack that influence, but the ultimate purpose of such efforts is to demystify, to show how charisma is a ruse of power just as Christianity is an opiate of the masses. *Normative* is not quite the right word for this sort of scholarly orientation, for it is not so much about oughts as it is about ought nots. In other words, it appears now that there are two ways of approaching charisma: descriptively, with the sociologist, or negatively, with the cultural theorist. What if we approach charisma with the full range of a normative palate? If we are interested in making the world more just, should we not probe for both the good and the bad, both the true and the false, both the ugly and the beautiful?

My project in this book is to develop this richer normative palate. In doing so, I transgress the boundaries between the sacred and the secular, the descriptive and the prescriptive, the cultural and the ethical. In one sense, I am engaged in conceptual analysis, and I conclude that charisma actually refers to two distinct concepts, authoritarian charisma and democratic charisma. In another sense, I am engaged in phenomenology, suspending the conceptual vocabulary that we would naturally apply to a scenario in order to allow the phenomenon to show itself, only then characterizing charisma. In yet another sense, I am engaged in a normative project, arguing that one type of charisma ought to be avoided and another ought to be appreciated. What this book does not do is offer a history. I work with the intuition that charisma is part of what it means to be human—indeed, I argue charisma names the display or concealment of the human—and so charisma is to be found in all human communities, far and near, recent and ancient. This is not a claim I seek to prove here. Rather, I show how charisma can be understood as closely connected with the meaning of the human through theoretical reflection and case studies, of Moses and of three works of twentieth-century American literature. I invite others to extend, complicate, or challenge this account with the insights they bring from studying other places and other times.

The argument of this book is that charisma comes in two forms, democratic charisma and authoritarian charisma. The failure to distinguish these two types of charisma has caused much confusion in the scholarly and popular discussion of charisma. It is this ambiguity that prompts the question, is charisma moral? My answer is yes for one type, no for another. Authoritarian charisma confirms social hierarchies and reinforces the powers that be. It is associated with fathers, with law, and with enchantment. Authoritarian charisma gives an audience what that audience desires. In contrast, democratic charisma invites an audience to develop new desires. Democratic charisma uses the words, images, and performances characteristic of a community to underscore the contingency and limitations of those words, images, and performances. Democratic charisma exposes the human by displaying how the human can never be perfectly represented. In doing so, democratic charisma challenges the powers that be. It points to the limits of law and calls us to a higher sense of justice. Democratic charisma is contagious: by displaying humanity it calls witnesses to explore their own humanity, calls them to refuse to see themselves in the way that the world sees them—and calls them to become charismatic themselves. Celebrity usually brings with it a form of authoritarian charisma, fulfilling superficial desires but ultimately concealing the human in layer upon layer of mediation, each of which magnifies the next. It is only on rare occasions that celebrities, actors, or politicians short-circuit these layers of mediation and so express the human, something that can only be shown through the failure of representation (as Judith Butler has elegantly put it). This is democratic charisma: it attracts and intrigues, and it calls an audience to respond not by ceding judgment but by asking new questions. We are all familiar with such democratic charisma, but it is rarely celebrated. It is found in the neighbor, the cousin, or the colleague. It is always imperfect, and it is often short-lived, but it reminds us of the best in the world, of the good, the true, and the beautiful, and it calls us toward justice.

One common answer to the question, is charisma moral?, is that what matters about charisma is how the extraordinary gifts it describes are used. If charisma just names extraordinary gifts, the morality of charisma would depend on the use of those gifts. A gifted orator could move audiences to do good or that orator could move audiences to do evil. On this account, charisma itself is morally neutral, just describing a feature of the world, those extraordinary gifts. I think this is the wrong way to address charisma's morality. Certainly, there are individuals who possess extraordinary gifts, but charisma names something different from the mere possession of such gifts. Indeed, the account of charisma I develop deemphasizes the extraordinary nature of such gifts just as it deemphasizes seemingly extraordinary individuals. In a sense, the most extraordinary gift of all is the fact of our humanity, and it is in the exposure or concealment of this gift that I find charisma operative. When charisma is recognized in both the neighbor and the autocrat, both the gym teacher and the rock star, we begin to realize that charisma has to do with a mode of self-presentation—and we begin to envision ways that charisma of the good sort, the democratic sort, might be cultivated. Like all virtues, charisma comes more easily to some than to others, and a select few are held up as exemplars, but all are able to recognize and cultivate democratic charisma. However, the extraordinary is important for my account of charisma because it is in the juxtaposition of ordinary and extraordinary that democratic charisma is capable of exposing the human, and inviting witnesses to interrogate the human in themselves. In contrast, authoritarian charisma uses the extraordinary to sanctify the ordinary, smoothing surfaces into an appealing shine that masks rather than solicits the human.

Before developing my own account of charisma in the chapters that follow, let us first reflect on the reasons that charisma has fallen into disrepute. Why do critics and scholars look on charisma with such suspicion? These criticisms are made plausible, I would suggest, by the failure to distinguish democratic from authoritarian charisma. While these criticisms are primarily directed at authoritarian charisma, they also hint at the possibilities for an alternative, democratic account of charisma.

The word that deflates every attempt to praise charisma, or even just to think carefully about charisma, is *Hitler*. Whether from television documentaries, *Triumph of the Will*, or *The Great Dictator*, images of Hitler's charisma are inescapable. Or at least we are tempted to call what we see charisma; it is a specific type of charisma, authoritarian charisma. What we see are many, many entranced faces, cut with a passionate, confident speaker. He speaks and the crowd roars and salutes. His lofty words about Germany and its great future are delivered crisply, his arms animated but not uncontrolled. Charisma names the apparent magic connecting speaker and audience. It names that which enchants. Hitler's charisma does not derive from the words he is saying, or from his vocal inflections or arm movements, or from his responsiveness to his audience. It is all these components together in a Gestalt that seems aptly named charisma. Leni Riefenstahl's cinematography in *Triumph of the Will* intuitively understands and magnifies this Gestalt, positioning the viewer not only as participant but as über-participant. To straightforwardly represent charisma on film, C-Span-style, would mean losing the charisma. The slow, circular pans of Riefenstahl's camera do more than mediate. They resonate with their content and so amplify it, amplify Hitler's charisma.

In Chaplin's parodic portrayal, everything is too much: the crowd responds too quickly, Hitler's arms and voice move too sharply, and finally, in the denouement, the previously overserious Hitler bleeds pathos. Chaplin does not show the man behind the mask. He understands that Hitler is not a performer; Hitler's speech is not a charismatic charade. Hitler's charisma does not derive from the man playing someone else. His charisma derives from the specificity of who he is even though who he is, Hitler, is always already mediated by the cultural waters in which he swims. Hitler is an ordinary, idiosyncratic individual who elicits ecstatic responses as that ordinariness is brought together with an extraordinary ability to encapsulate the desires of a community. But this display is delicate. As soon as it falls back on familiar cultural tropes packaged in a familiar way by an ordinary man, the enchantment of charisma is gone. That is why Chaplin succeeds: he undermines Hitler's charisma by unpackaging the charismatic Gestalt and distending each component. Now we see a bad actor or an absurd man, and those enchanted must be mad. At the film's conclusion, Chaplin's Hitler ends his performance, and he is redeemed. Beneath the actor is a man whose humanity is soft and sensitive.

Because Hitler is so identified with charisma, charisma becomes identified with evil, or the threat of evil. We come to think of charisma as performance that seduces. The charismatic speaker is a Don Juan for the masses, entrancing listeners in order to advance his or her own interests. These interests range from the self-aggrandizing to the world-historical. Followers of the charismatic leader are so smitten that they lose their heads. Reason is suppressed as pure emotion, pure misguided affection, takes its place. The only reasons that followers will give for their commitment to the charismatic leader are echoes of the reasons offered by the charismatic leader, no matter how unreasonable those may be. What could be more evil than denying others the capacity to be themselves, to reason and feel as they naturally would? In an age so enamored with dialogue, with exchanging reasons and critically dissecting arguments and even bringing emotions into the realm of reason (an unreasonable love, an irrational fear), charisma runs sharply against contemporary values.

The connection between dangerous seduction and political charisma runs deep, and it is reinforced when both are linked with the religious. A glitzy preacher displays the superficiality and dangers of charisma, offering something to believe in, really something to feel a part of, while transparently (from the perspective of the cynical secularist) displaying how faith in him translates into wealth for him. Such a translation is, of course, also the case with movie stars and the famous more generally, but it is never clearer than in the case of the prosperity gospel preacher with his fancy car, sparkling rings, and smart suits. Flannery O'Connor powerfully captures this dynamic on a small scale in her story "Good Country People." A Bible salesman seduces the protagonist, a one-legged philosopher living with her mother in the country, through a performance of ignorance combined with faith. The protagonist, a sad, bookish woman who has changed her name from Joy to Hulga, believes herself to be taking advantage of the Bible salesman, none too subtly named Manley Pointer. Once Manley and Hulga are in her hayloft, the seduction quickly transforms from kisses to religious revelation. Manley's Bible box contains wicked things: alcohol, pornography, and playing cards. Manley steals Hulga's false leg and leaves her in the hayloft. Even the philosopher, perhaps especially the philosopher, is liable to seduction at once religious and sexual. O'Connor presents Hulga as a paradigmatic critical thinker, self-reflective in a way that those "good country people" around her were not. Manley is presented as the opposite of charismatic: he seems innocent, fragile, and provincial. But the climax of the story reveals charisma where it seemed there was none; or, rather, it reveals how charisma combines the ordinary and the extraordinary. Hulga is driven by emotion that mutes her critical capacities, and she comes face to face with evil. Charisma is presented as disingenuous performance—the ordinary dressed up as extraordinary—that seduces with its ultimately phallic power.

There are, of course, women described as charismatic, but in such cases the connotation of charisma is not so clearly evil because the seduction is more conventional. According to convention, the woman is beautiful or smart or both and attracts men who desire her. These men may lose their mind in love, but they are motivated by a selfish goal: sexual conquest. Perhaps it is this gendered view of seduction that makes us represent charismatic men as evil. Either the seduction by the male charismatic results in an uncomfortable male desire for men, in the case of the male follower, or it results in the threat that women, already prone to irrationality in love, will abandon their lovers to follow the charismatic leader. O'Connor's story suggests that even the most apparently frigid women are liable to be seduced by the sexual-religious power of charisma.

If, in the popular imagination, Hitler always taints charisma, the best retort is Martin Luther King, Jr. Yet King's charisma is not usually what is described as King's praiseworthy feature. It is King himself who is essentially good, and because of that goodness he is able to put charisma, a talent with which he happened to be gifted, to good use. King's vocation was to preach. He came from a family of Southern ministers and he himself began preaching early, in his teens. Far and away the most iconic images of King represent his preaching, most powerfully in American cultural memory at the March on Washington in 1963. King used his charisma, his gift for oratory, to transform the national conscience. He was able to introduce and advance a novel idea, that a principled commitment to nonviolence could affect dramatic social change. As the story goes, while there were many civil rights leaders, both during King's day and before, the end of segregation came because of King's charisma. He had a *je ne sais quoi* that touched whites as well as blacks, the young as well as the old, Northerners as well as Southerners. If Hitler muted his listeners' reason, compelling them to do evil, King also muted the reason of his listeners, but this was a good thing. The reasoning of Americans in those days was deeply flawed, encrusted by tradition or hopelessness. There were many reasons given for segregation, and for acceding to segregation.

What was needed to end segregation was not a rigorous examination of those reasons but an occasion to set them aside, an occasion to open oneself to new possibilities for living together.

This story of King the charismatic is rather romantic, and rather fanciful. If a concession is made to the complications of reality, it is to acknowledge that King the man was flawed, like all human beings, even though he was gifted. What we should pay attention to and learn from is his greatness, the way his oratory captured the heart of a nation, not the details of his personal life. In other words, what matters about King is his charisma. On the other hand, more skeptical critics have found King's charisma to be his most problematic feature. Essentially, King's charisma is distracting, and it is compromised. It is distracting because it diverts our attention from the actual engine of social change, the actual cause of segregation's demise: community organizing among blacks in the South. Organizing is far less glamorous than speech-giving. Holding community meetings, soliciting resources, building relationships, strategizing, and pushing against a seemingly impenetrable opposition cannot be captured in sound bites, and it is of limited interest to newspaper reporters. But it is the work of ordinary people, often women, collectively, both intensively in the 1950s and 1960s and gradually over the decades that came before, that altered the social landscape of the South. If the civil rights movement is remembered as King speaking, it will provide an ineffective model for those seeking social justice in the present. They will imagine themselves spectators rather than actors, waiting for a racial messiah. Another worry about King's charisma is that it is deeply dependent on the media even as King's interests could be quite different from the interests of the media. King achieved fame through media reports of the protests, marches, and speeches in which he participated. The media wanted to tell a story with a singular protagonist, and the story often was presented as a story about King rather than a story about a movement. Even if King did not want the focus to be on himself, the spotlight on a single leader was an inevitable part of the genre. Instead of reporting on the issues, television stations were tempted to report on King's charisma, offering his oratory as a sort of entertainment that distracted from the moral significance of the cause in which it was employed. The media-fueled attention showered on a single leader could turn dangerous. As soon as that leader falls into media disfavor, as soon as a blemish appears on the record of the man presented as so saintly, the movement for which he stands loses momentum.

Now that years have passed since the 2008 presidential campaign, it is easy to forget that Barack Obama was once presented as possessing King-like charisma. That Obama was cast in this role was made possible in part by the way he comfortably fit into a tradition of black male leadership, from Marcus Garvey and Malcolm X to Martin Luther King, Jr., and Jessie Jackson. Skeptical scholars suggest that what is at work in such figures is not so much charisma as it is a style of performance, a scenario. A heterosexual black man leads the masses, and intrigues white onlookers. Ella Baker, Anna Julia Cooper, and Flo Kennedy could speak compellingly and move their listeners to action, but because of their gender or sexuality they could not participate in the standard model of black leadership and so never had the kind of following of Malcolm X or Martin Luther King, Jr. In an important sense, the substance of what Obama said and even the way that he said it had little to do with his charisma, skeptical critics would charge. He played a role, in part through his own embrace of that role and in part through the media's appetite for a leader who could play that role. It is a role of specifically *black* leadership, and it does not translate particularly well into national political leadership—a style of performance with its own repertoire of roles and styles. After his election, Obama could no longer be framed as a leader of blacks, and very quickly the media and its consumers forgot that Obama was supposed to be charismatic. In other words, Obama did not lose charisma because of the nuts and bolts of governing. He lost charisma because he was cast to play one sort of charismatic leader (black) but was unable to find his bearings as another sort of charismatic leader (presidential). Indeed, presidential charisma—of a Clinton, Reagan, or Roosevelt—is a role reserved for white actors. Charisma would seem to name a certain style of performance into which only certain actors can be cast, with the parameters set by the media and the historical story it constructs.

While one line of attack on charisma charges that the charismatic leader is dependent on the media or on a certain repertoire of charismatic performance in order to be recognized as charismatic, another line of attack goes even further. On this view, charisma is simply a catalyst for ideology. There are certain ideas that a culture shares, ideas that advance the interests of that culture's elite at the expense of those who are on the margins. For example, a particular understanding of freedom as essential to the American way of life. Freedom must mean lack of constraints on an individual's financial decisions. This definition advances the interests of those who are so wealthy that they do not need resources to be shared across a community for health care, child care, legal aid, education, and so on, shared resources that can only be offered by taxation. Ideological work is necessary to convince a poor person that taxes should be lowered on the rich: that freedom should be defined in a particular way advancing the interests of the few at the expense of the many. How does such work happen? Clearly the educational system is one way in which ideology is made to seem natural and unquestionable. Ideology also circulates in conversations between family members, colleagues, and neighbors, but this is still not enough to explain how ideas that advance the interests of others could be adopted as one's own. It is only those who are somehow entranced who could commit themselves to such ideas, and it is charisma that entrances, according to charisma's critics. This is charisma in a broad sense: it includes the charisma of the schoolteacher, structurally positioned as expert; the charisma of the father, bringing the child into a world of norms; the charisma of the politician, relying on established political tropes; and the charisma of the celebrity, regurgitating rather than challenging the dominant ideas of a culture.

Oprah's charisma exemplifies what these ideology critics worry about. Magnified by her multimedia presence, not only on television and in film but also in magazines and websites, Oprah attracts and enchants. Her charisma is deeper than mere performance: it is impossible to imagine Oprah not being Oprah. Indeed, it is Oprah's sincerity that solidifies her charisma. It is a sincerity that extends to a perceived desire to make her audience better, to allow each individual to live to his or her fullest potential, just as Oprah does. The means by which this potential is to be realized is consumption: buying the right products, reading the right books, viewing the right shows (not least of them Oprah's, but now a broader range of shows on her cable network). In a sense, Oprah has charisma at its purest because her charisma comes about through performing the ideas she communicates. She is charismatic insofar as she elicits a desire in the viewer to be like her, to join the ranks of the charismatic. But doing this requires a certain understanding of the self (always to be improved) and the world (always to be consumed) that allows for Oprah's performances to be taken as charismatic and that is communicated through her performances. These ideas about self and world are ideology: they are the ideas circulating in American, now global, culture, catalyzed by the likes of Oprah, that advance the interests of the wealthy and the powerful—like Oprah herself.

That Oprah can become a prime example of charisma points to another worry of charisma's critics. Today, they charge, charisma and celebrity are confused. When our experience of charisma is largely mediated through newspaper, television, or film, when the experience of standing in a crowd witnessing a charismatic speaker has been eclipsed by the structured charisma of TED talks viewed on a mobile phone, charisma becomes closely identified with fame. When we do meet famous people, they automatically seem charismatic because the role of the famous person is to be charismatic. Anyone whose YouTube video has been viewed hundreds of thousands of times becomes a celebrity, and the reason that their video was watched so often must have something to do with charisma. To thrive in the media world, as a television personality or a movie actor, it is necessary to elicit feelings in an audience that seem quite similar to those elicited by the charismatic. Of course the major difference has been that the media personality is self-consciously performing, following a repertoire of established practices (in the case of a TED talk speaker, a quite tightly managed style of performance). Contemporary fame drifts away from charisma since charisma, as it has been classically understood, is about the exceptional individual, not the exceptional performance and not exceptional fame. Charisma is about who someone is, not what someone does.

Yet this distinction between the person and her performances may be unsustainable. Charisma may not always have been mediated through television, film, or mobile phones, but charisma has always been mediated, and those with charisma have been those whose personality somehow resonates with the available media, amplifying their natural gifts. It is hard to imagine a silent charismatic: both words and voice are media through which charisma flows. Various amplification technologies began when Moses, a founding figure of charisma, used his brother Aaron as the medium through which to communicate. (Moses himself stuttered.) Evidence of charisma that now circulates online once circulated through newspapers and, earlier still, through hearsay. For the critic of charisma, such inescapable mediation taints the concept of charisma. When charisma is mediated, it is harder to understand charisma as possessed by a gifted individual; it is tempting to see the medium itself as setting the criteria for charisma. Charisma in an age of YouTube would seem to be a different phenomenon than charisma in an age of newspapers.

The opposite worry about charisma is also compelling. If charisma is not understood as always mediated, charisma must be otherworldly. Charisma must require a belief in the supernatural. In a world of representation upon representation, charisma interrupts from the outside. One of the histories told about the word *charisma* traces it back to early Christianity when the disciples of Jesus received divine gifts. This usage continues in Pentecostalism, where speaking in tongues is the quintessential gift of the Spirit, an eruption of the divine into the human world. Such gifts always remain opaque; all attempts to represent them fall short, just as all attempts to represent God in human language fall short. When a churchgoer begins speaking in tongues, her fellows recognize that a divine gift is present but they are unable to understand exactly what the content of this gift may be (though a translation may be posited). From this opacity the content becomes the presence of the gift itself and nothing

more. Indeed, charisma, or charisms as they are called in contemporary Christian communities, indicates a site of pure presence, a place where all the mediations and representations that
so characterize our world short-circuit. While the specifically
Christian usage of *charisma* has developed independently from
the term's broader usage, the sense that a transcendent gift is
involved is characteristic of this broader usage as well. Even
film stars deemed particularly charismatic are often described
as having a certain indescribable, otherworldly gift: think Greta
Garbo, Cary Grant, Audrey Hepburn, or Marilyn Monroe.
Giftedness is even more a part of how musical charisma is
represented: think Elvis Presley, Nina Simone, perhaps Amy
Winehouse, to name but a few. The talent and "presence" of
such figures are seen as superhuman, as necessarily originating
from the beyond. The individuals themselves are quite ordinary,
with parents and complicated personal lives and imperfections,
but they also have something else. In other words, the ordinary is
not molded toward the extraordinary; the ordinary and the extraordinary coexist, the extraordinary an ineffable gift supple-
menting the ordinary. Critical inquiry and scholarship along
these lines strive to reveal the ordinary individual to counter the
overdetermination of the extraordinary. Marilyn Monroe is
thought of as gifted in her ability to portray female sensuality,
but as Jacqueline Rose has persuasively shown Monroe also enjoyed reading serious literature and thinking critically about the
world. In other words, the job of the critic becomes suspending
the possibility of divine gift and exploring the charismatic figure
apart from her gift of charisma.

Another worry: All of this talk of divine gifts sounds quite
mysterious, the language of religious seekers and New Age en-
thusiasts, if not Christian theologians. The work of the critic or
scholar is to explain such knots of mystery, not to admire them.

Charisma must be the language of fans or the faithful, the claim of giftedness obscuring the thousands of hours of practice and the many precedents for any apparent encounter with pure presence, with magical performance. Describing Hitler or King as charismatic might be appropriate language for a television documentary, but it is ultimately language that further enchants: the ascription of charisma is inextricable from the layers of representation of the charisma itself. To talk about a divine gift is to invoke the rhetoric of charisma, a rhetoric that persuades and conceals like all appeals to the transcendent. Indeed, such rhetoric can be particularly invidious where it reinforces existing social hierarchies: what seems like a divine gift might only be accessible to heterosexual males, to take the example of the apparent gift of the black leader.

This worry about the supposed transcendence of charisma can also be framed diachronically, as understandings of transcendence change through history. Weber's foundational account of charisma relies on such historical change—not change in what transcendence is but change in how transcendence is understood. Once, long ago or far away, communities easily accepted that certain of their members were given special gifts by the gods. This was a reason to listen to them, to appreciate their gifts, and in some cases to follow them. As time passed, as we entered modernity, the mysteries of the world receded as science advanced. Societies became more systematically organized: academies developed the talent of young musicians, politicians studied political science and worked their way up through the political system, and government bureaucracy put emphasis on following rules instead of following leaders. On this view, charisma may have played a significant social role at a distance, temporal and geographical, from the modern West, but charisma no longer plays a role in our world.

What of the people who seem charismatic today? Critics may charge that they seem charismatic, but they do not have the authority that classically accompanies charisma. In the past, encountering someone with charismatic authority meant ceding our own capacity to judge to the charismatic figure. This does not seem to happen substantially with, for example, ostensibly charismatic musicians or movie stars. They may be admired, but we do not defer to their judgment (with the exception, perhaps, of product endorsements). If we are sick, we defer to the judgment of a doctor; if we wonder about Mars, we defer to the judgment of an astronomer. But in our democratic moment, we are very wary of deferring to the judgment of politicians. Indeed, they ought to defer to our judgment: the people, collectively, are authoritative, and it is to us, not to any one individual, that deference is owed. Our world is closed off from the supernatural, fully explicable in terms of science and reason, so there is no place for charisma anymore. On this view, with modernity charisma reduces to celebrity, offering entertainment rather than guidance. From the perspective of this secularization story, one need not believe that God was really acting in the world before or outside of modernity. It is just that people thought it possible for the transcendent to shine through the world, so they thought it reasonable to defer to the judgment of charismatic figures. Our modern world receives no such light from the transcendent. What is good, what is true, and what is beautiful are determined instrumentally, based on worldly interests— what is good for us, true for us, beautiful for us. This secularization story either reduces us humans to crudely mechanistic creatures, no different than animals or rocks, or implicitly relies on the view that humans have a particular attunement to the good, the true, and the beautiful. Charismatic leaders are not necessary to do what we can do for ourselves. The argument developed in this book agrees that ordinary people are naturally attuned to the good, the true, and the beautiful, but such attunement is often suppressed by cultural and ideological forces. Charisma at its best, democratic charisma rather than authoritarian charisma, restores this natural attunement.

The community organizing tradition of Saul Alinsky has a saying: the goal of an organizer is find her replacements. The organizer shows others that they are capable of becoming leaders, that they are capable of articulating who they are beyond what the world tells them, and they are capable of mobilizing their neighbors and colleagues to work collectively toward justice. When an organizer comes into a community, she uses democratic charisma to prompt community members to reflect on their own problems and concerns, reflection that is usually suppressed by the inertia of our ordinary modes of seeing the world and seeing ourselves. The organizer uses words, symbols, and performances familiar to that community but in a way that is unfamiliar. Alinsky writes of the Judeo-Christian heritage of America as fundamentally radical; he calls for a dramatic reordering of American society around the interests of those who are disempowered, but he distances himself from "ideologies" such as Communism. Alinsky and his followers were always outsiders to the communities that they attempted to organize, but the role of outsider is often conducive to democratic charisma. It is difficult for the insider to escape overdetermination, to have anything other than authoritarian charisma. The insider who gathers a following is often seen as embodying the values of a community, and she often gains standing by fulfilling her community's desires in familiar ways—desires for a father figure, for a strong voice, or for wide learning. Alinsky, who explicitly aligns himself with the outsider-organizing efforts of that ancient prototype of charisma, Moses, positions himself not as a great man but as quintessentially human. He swears, tells jokes, and gets his hands dirty with practicalities; what he does not do is bring specific goals or policy proposals. He brings an expansive vision of democracy led by the have-nots, and that vision captivates. Alinsky's audience is intrigued by his democratic vision, but their desires are not sated by proposals he brings to the table. They are forced to look within themselves to examine what desires they have that have not yet been expressed, human desires repressed by dehumanizing conditions. Once those desires begin to be expressed, community members realize that others have these same desires, and that collective action could challenge the forces of dehumanization wielded by the powers that be.

America offers a particularly well-suited site for reflecting on charisma because its democratic ethos allows for extraordinary gifts to appear and be welcomed everywhere, not just among an elite. Americans are primed to respond to democratic charisma, but democratic charisma is rarely celebrated. What is celebrated is authoritarian charisma. In the American imagination, charismata, divine gifts, are not bestowed upon hereditary powers. Rather, it is hard work leading to social or monetary ascent that is seen as marking divine gifts: Steve Jobs, Warren Buffett, Barack Obama, Donald Trump, and so on. To defer to the authority of such figures is to solidify the powers that be: the narratives of their lives that earn them charismatic authority fit comfortably with the American narratives that secure social hierarchy—work hard and you will be rewarded, and you will show that you are blessed. There is another way that authoritarian charisma is presented in America: through the celebrity. From Clint Eastwood to Brad Pitt, from Katherine Hepburn to Meryl Streep, from Oprah to the Kardashians, Americans look to celebrities with reverence. Most often, these celebrities achieve

their fame because of the ease with which that fame can be represented and magnified by mass media, fulfilling the desires of
an audience. (It is significant that we think of talented actors as
necessarily charismatic while extraordinarily talented chess play-
ers, for example, may or may not be charismatic.) Such figures,
however, do not seem to have the authority often thought to
accompany charisma. They may be revered, but do Americans
cede their judgment to the judgment of a celebrity? Perhaps not
often, but the celebrity product endorsement is an important
exception, suggesting the close connection between charisma
and capitalism. Even when celebrities are seemingly committed
to doing good, for example, after a natural disaster, this often
comes in the form of soliciting monetary contributions. Despite
the prominence of celebrities in American culture, the second
most admired man or woman as determined by the annual
Gallup poll of Americans is someone almost never described as
having charisma. This person, more admired than Pope Francis, more admired than Angelina Jolie, is what the poll lists as
"friend/relative." In other words, there is a robust undercurrent
of democratic charisma in America, writ small, even though it
receives little media attention.

This book begins with Moses, seemingly a paradigm of charisma, and one particularly important for American self-understanding. When the story of Moses is read carefully, what first
appeared to be authoritarian charisma turns out to be democratic charisma. Moses did not embody the values and traditions of the Israelites and command them with a thundering
voice. He was an outsider, he stuttered, and his message was
always mediated—first through Aaron, who spoke to the Israelites for him, and then through layer upon layer of religious
commentary and, more recently, through cinematic representation. The book then responds to skepticism about charisma by

developing, in the next chapter, the distinction between authoritarian and democratic charisma. Democratic charisma is presented as a virtue, and it is developed through meditations on closely connected phenomena, including idols and icons, lovers and parents, and media and cultural mediation. The next three chapters turn to three American literary texts about race, a theme at the core of the American experience and a theme that puts into relief the possibilities and limitations of charisma for doing justice. That these are literary texts is not a convenience or a disciplinary convention. One of the central arguments of this book is that mediation is essential to charisma: democratic charisma calls attention to the limits of mediation while authoritarian charisma conceals mediation to create the illusion of pure presence. Engaging with literary texts acknowledges and provides an opportunity to explore this centrality of mediation. These three chapters are organized by the themes of goodness, truth, and beauty: democratic charisma opens the world to what is beyond the world by using the inescapability of mediation against itself. Each of these chapters also emphasizes the fugitive nature of democratic charisma, always but a few steps away from capture by the powers that be. The conclusion reflects on the ways democratic charisma advances justice, and the ways authoritarian charisma naturalizes injustice. The narrative arc of the book is meant to challenge the association of charisma with great men, opening us to the democratic charisma we are already familiar with, but we rarely recognize, in our friends, neighbors, and colleagues. Charisma is not inherently problematic; in fact, it can be emancipatory. It is patriarchy, racism, and capitalism that are the problems, and they have caused great confusion about charisma. Charisma can support those evils, but it can also combat them.

A note on terminology is necessary. While the book generally attempts to avoid technical language and to take the ways in which charisma is ordinarily represented as a starting point, three key concepts may seem obscure. Their repetition and development in different contexts should increase clarity as the book progresses, but here is a place to start with each. First, I use *the human* to mark that part of our humanity that cannot be accurately described by the world or even by our self. It marks who we are rather than what we are. *Inwardness* refers to the awareness of this excess, but it should be understood as pointing to intrigue rather than answers. The term *humanity* suggests qualities that all people share; *the human* suggests that what each person shares is what cannot be expressed in a list of qualities. Democratic charisma makes visible the human; authoritarian charisma conceals it. Mediation is essential to charisma. Sometimes I use *mediation* interchangeably with the rather inelegant term *cultural substance* because *mediation* refers to the words, images, and performances that are characteristic of a culture—really, that make up a culture. *Mediation* includes media, the vehicles that transport words, images, and performances, and mass media, the high-speed, hi-tech means of such transportation, including television and the Internet. I also sometimes use *mediation* interchangeably with *representation* because what words, images, and performances do is represent: they stand in for something else. To ignore mediation is to embrace the myth of pure presence, the belief that we can encounter our world or our self without relying on the words, images, and performances of our culture. Finally, the term *charisma* itself needs clarification. Democratic charisma expresses the human, so there is always a person who is charismatic. Authoritarian charisma conceals the human; objects, animals, and people (dehumanized) can have authoritarian charisma. Sometimes I refer to a *charismatic performance*; this runs against the intuition that it is a person rather than a performance that is charismatic. I do not mean to imply that charisma is an act put on for an audience. By *charismatic performance* I simply call attention to a particular moment when the dynamics of charisma are particularly visible: whether the human is revealed or concealed, whether mediation is embraced or short-circuited.

A note on sources is also necessary. Many scholars and critics have written about charisma, and even more have written important work on topics closely related to charisma. In this book's afterword, I develop my argument about democratic charisma through a critical engagement with some of this scholarship. The afterword also serves as a bibliographical essay, offering the reader pointers to the works that have informed my thinking on these topics (and full citations). This is not a comprehensive guide to what has been written about charisma. Rather, it is a path through the literature that functions as something like the obverse of the preceding argument, situating my thoughts in traditions and offering some reflections on how those traditions are advanced, or challenged, by the account of democratic charisma developed here. Because charisma is relevant to numerous disciplines—political theory, performance studies, literature, cultural studies, ethics, religious studies, and theology, to name a few—as well as a topic of interest beyond the academy, it made more sense to generally set various scholarly debates aside until the end.

A special cautionary note must be offered to those readers interested in the specifically Christian sense of charisma, sometimes appropriated in comparative studies of religion. This book is not about charisma as it is found in Christian worship, or as it is venerated in traditions such as Pentecostalism. There is much fruitful thinking that could be done along these lines, connecting secular, sociological, and cultural discussions of charisma with discussions of charisma as part of pneumatology, theological study of the Holy Spirit. This is a project for others, but perhaps this book, with its emphasis on the normative dimensions of charisma, could open a path for such projects to take. When charisma as it appears in culture orients to the good, the true, and the beautiful, it is easy to see how theologians could interpret the gifts of the Spirit similarly, both within and beyond a formal church setting. Scholars of comparative religion, at least those not too allergic to the language of normativity, may find the categories of democratic charisma and authoritarian charisma useful; indeed, even though they are developed here in a normative framework, they could be described without that framework—for example, by leaning on the distinction between fulfilling the desires of an audience and creating new desires in an audience.

Does charisma disappear in a secular world, in a world emptied of religious presence? This book argues that rather than thinking in terms of immanence and transcendence, enchantment and disenchantment, presence and absence, we ought to think in terms of modes of mediation. The networks of words, images, and performances, flowing through media, accelerated by technology, that pervade the West today are different than those in the West a century or a millennium ago, and they are different than those in other corners of the world. But the hypothesis that I want to make plausible through the chapters that follow is that charisma is to be found in them all, and that charisma names the visibility of the human in a network of mediation. The human interrupts the supposed smoothness of mediation, and it solicits more interruptions. But when it is the simulacrum of the human that appears, when it is authoritarian charisma, the hold that our mediated world has on us tightens, and those whose interests are served by these networks of mediation are secured in their status. At the end of the day, democratic charisma is a challenge to the powers that be, a voice that is both familiar and strange, drawing our attention to mediation and calling us toward justice.

1

THE UNCIRCUMCISED LIPS
OF MOSES

Who could offer a better image of charisma than Moses? Standing strong and tall, living righteously, speaking to God, leading a people who respect his extraordinary gifts—this is what charisma is supposed to look like. Of course, this is not Moses but Charlton Heston playing Moses in the extravagant film *The Ten Commandments*, released in 1956. Filmed in Egypt and directed by Cecil B. DeMille, lasting three and a half hours, an astronomical financial success, *The Ten Commandments* is quintessential Hollywood, and quintessential charisma. It makes charisma into Hollywood charisma, and into American charisma. It is shown annually on American television at Easter, and it continues to offer the model for cinematic depictions of Moses, including, most recently, the DreamWorks animated *Prince of Egypt* (1998) and the Ridley Scott–directed *Exodus: Gods and Kings* (2014), featuring Christian Bale as Moses. Both closely follow the filmic vocabulary developed by DeMille. In each, Moses is a classic Hollywood hero, projecting masculinity, power, and eloquence. As a baby, his Jewish mother must send him away so that he is not killed by Pharaoh's orders. He is adopted into Pharaoh's household, his identity a secret, and he pleases Pharaoh greatly, even more than Pharaoh's biological son, Rameses. Eventually, Moses learns of his adoptive origins. He grows frustrated with the Egyptians' oppression of the Jews, kills an Egyptian taskmaster, and flees or is exiled. Eventually, he returns, rallies the Jewish people with the help of miracles performed by God, and leads the Jews out of Egypt. Then, he receives God's law and gives it to the Jewish people.

The Ten Commandments opens with an announcement (quite literally: the director steps out onto a stage to read it) that the film depicts the contrast between unjust, worldly law and a new law, God's law. The film is strikingly Christian: the Jewish people are hoping for a savior to release them from the shackles imposed by the old law, Pharaoh's law. Moses is this savior, proclaiming that the old law no longer needs to be followed and that a new law comes directly from God. The film is also strikingly American. In addition to the instantly recognizable Hollywood conventions and American accents, Exodus is framed as a story of nation-building, a story of a people leaving oppression and moving to a new land where they would be free, where there would be justice. Exodus is the American Revolution, Moses is the Founding Father, and the Ten Commandments are the Constitution. America *is* Judeo-Christian, nation and religion are one and the same. It takes a great man with great faith and great gifts to lead the new nation; Americans should be proud of their great men, should model themselves on great men, or on the followers of great men.

While the Exodus story has greatly appealed to black Americans and became a key community-building text for them, it is whites who suffer injustice in the cinematic depictions of Exodus. Yet *The Ten Commandments*, released during the Montgomery Bus Boycott, must certainly have primed American media for a depiction of the civil rights movement, and particu-

larly Martin Luther King, Jr., as mobilizing a religiously motivated, oppressed community seeking freedom. King himself
would embrace this identification. In his last speech, the night
before his assassination, he cites Moses's final scene in the Bible.
King, like Moses, has seen the promised land from afar, he is
confident his people are moving toward it, but he doubts he
himself will reach the land of milk and honey. The tendency to
read the civil rights movement through the Exodus narrative
was felt particularly by black Student Nonviolent Coordinating
Committee leader Bob Moses, whose name, and likely his own
charisma, led to such unrealistic expectations from the communities in which he worked that for a time Moses would use
his mother's maiden name, becoming Robert Parris. It is tempting to read the more than two centuries of black American ap-
propriation of the Exodus narrative through the lens of *The
Ten Commandments*, and to worry that a troublingly masculine,
American, and authoritarian style of leadership has always
dominated the black political imagination. In other words, it is
tempting to imagine Moses as Charlton Heston instead of engaging with the biblical text itself. It is tempting to reduce Exodus to a great (white) man freeing the slaves.

Charlton Heston's Moses fulfills the desires of the Israelites,
desires constituted by their time in bondage. They long for a
leader with the strength and power of Pharaoh, and Heston's
Moses is precisely that—indeed, he nearly *was* Pharaoh. Heston's Moses is self-assured: he was a confident Egyptian leader
and then, as soon as he discovered his Israelite origins, he became
a confident Israelite leader, standing up to Egyptian oppression
as he disguises himself as a Jewish slave. Heston's Moses is a
powerful presence, speaking directly to his people and directly
to God. In contrast, the biblical Moses does not give the Israelites what they want. He leaves them supremely frustrated as

they impatiently wait for liberation to finally come, for the jour-
ney to the Promised Land to finally conclude. The biblical Moses hesitates and doubts and is unsure of his identity; he never
comfortably occupies the role of national leader. The most
striking and significant difference between Heston's Moses and
the Moses of the Book of Exodus is that the latter never communicates directly—not with God and not with the Israelites.
Moses is said to be ineloquent and to have "uncircumcised lips,"
often understood as a speech impediment, perhaps a stutter.
Mediation is essential to the Exodus story: God speaks to Moses,
who speaks to Aaron, who speaks to the Israelite elders, who
speak to the Israelite people—and this is all recorded in a text,
Exodus, layered with commentary and interpretation, projected
onto the movie screen, and eventually reaches us. In other words,
mediation is essential to Moses's charisma, but mediation must
not overdetermine Moses's charisma—we must not conflate
Moses and Heston. Reflection on the biblical narrative, and
particularly the evocative image of Moses's "uncircumcised lips,"
so different from Heston's muscular build and manly voice, offers a way to understand this relationship between charisma
and mediation. When mediation is ignored, Heston becomes
Moses (and America becomes Israel); when mediation is engaged
with, we begin to see the democratic potential of charisma,
always precarious but never absent.

In the biblical narrative, Moses's identity is essentially split.
He is both Egyptian and Jewish, in a sense too Egyptian to be
Jewish and too Jewish to be Egyptian. He is always a "foreigner
in a foreign land," but this does not mean that he is free of any
worldly attachments. Rather, it means that he is constantly
aware that who he is exceeds how the world sees him, exceeds
even how he can see himself. Every worldly description of him
will fall short. Unlike the cinematic depictions, Exodus does

not suggest that Moses's Israelite identity was ever concealed from him during his youth at Pharaoh's court. The narrative's silence suggests that Moses knew he was both of and not of Pharaoh's world from the start. There is no hint that the identity of Moses's mother was concealed from him: she was invited by Pharaoh's daughter to nurse and raise the young boy. This distance from Pharaoh is also significant. Whereas Hollywood makes Moses Pharaoh's adoptive son and potential heir, the relationship in the biblical narrative is more distant, and mediated through a woman, Pharaoh's daughter. Indeed, questions of lineage are essential to the biblical narrative. The book of Exodus itself begins with a list of the names of the Israelites who originally went to Egypt. Time passes, the Israelites multiply, and Pharaoh worries. He orders that their number be reduced, eventually resorting to condemning all Hebrew boys to death in the Nile. There is a threat that the lineage of the Israelites will be broken: tradition that passes from generation to generation, from father to son, will be halted with the death of the sons. Moses escapes this fate when his mother secrets him away, into Pharaoh's daughter's care. Moses thus represents a singular hope for the future of the Jewish people. It is a hope that is closely related to God's covenant with the people of Israel: God habitually identifies himself as "the God of your father, the God of Abraham, the God of Isaac, and the God of Jacob," naming the proximate father, then the first father, his son, and his grandson, the lineage of generations constitutive of the Israelite people. This centrality of generations is echoed in the final, decisive plague that God brings to the Egyptians. God kills all of the firstborn Egyptians while saving all of the firstborn Israelites who follow his orders to protect their homes. God is not just turning the tables on the Egyptians, doing to them what they did to the Israelites. He is challenging the symbol of their tradition, their peoplehood: the possibility for generational continuity, for a culture to pass down from father to (firstborn) son.

That Moses's identity is uncertain (and it is uncertain in the secondary literature as well, most famously in Freud's claim that Moses was not an Israelite at all) opens him to appreciating what is most essential in him, what is most human—which is also what is most divine. When God charges Moses with approaching Pharaoh, Moses demurs, "Who am I that I should go to Pharaoh, and bring the Israelites out of Egypt?" God responds, "I will be with you" (3:11–12). God does not name any attributes of Moses, does not say that he is strong or handsome or eloquent. God simply states that what qualifies Moses is that God will accompany him. This is, essentially, a reminder of what is obvious in the tradition: humans are created in the image of God. What makes a human being human is her likeness to God; if God is understood in the negative, as indescribable, then what makes the human being human is that which exceeds description or representation.

Moses hesitates often, but he ultimately obeys. He did not know who he was, but he discovers that rather than being what the world sees him as—an Egyptian at Pharaoh's court, an Israelite, or a member of his wife's community of Midianites—he should be content with being a follower of God. What does this mean, precisely? That is what Moses wants to know when he asks God for God's name. God responds with what is usually interpreted as an archaic form of the verb *to be*, stating, "I am who I am" (3:14). Who is God? That which exceeds any worldly representation, that which exceeds language, that which exceeds any list of descriptions, and that which has the effect of inviting others to ask who they are beyond the way the world describes them. When Moses later asks God, "Show me your ways, so I may know you and find favor in your sight" (33:13), God responds by offering to give Moses his Presence. There is no more to God than this, Presence without attributes, and it is by remembering this that Moses will be able to act in Godly ways. God invites the Israelites to see themselves as more than slaves. God tells Moses to tell the Israelites, "I am has sent me to you," evocatively equivocating between the irreducible name of God, "I am," and Moses's own identity, who Moses is beyond worldly descriptions (3:14). Here is the contagion of charisma: those who witness charisma and seek to respond do so by demonstrating, performing, their existence beyond worldly descriptions. The Israelites want a god who can be explained in their language, in their way of seeing the world. The God who appears to Moses can only be seen through failures of representation, through attempts to access God that are indirect and that inevitably, in the narrative, lead to confusion.

Moses appreciates the difficulties involved, and he resists God's charge. How can Moses accurately represent "I am"? "I have never been eloquent," "I am slow of speech and slow of tongue," he demurs (4:10). God will assist him, Moses is told. Moses imagines that charisma requires a thundering, persuasive voice that can appeal to the masses, telling the Israelites what they want to hear, and in a way that they want to hear it. Moses doubts again: "I am a poor speaker" in the English translation; "I am uncircumcised of lips" in the Hebrew (6:30). What this could mean remains unclear, with various interpretations put forward by scholars of the Hebrew Bible. It could be a lisp or a stutter. It could be that Moses, away from Egypt for many years, has forgotten the Egyptian language. The phrase certainly seems to suggest something quite different from conventional masculine strength. Instead of a powerful, persuasive tongue, Moses has lips that are unable to command.

Circumcision, after all, makes a Jewish man. The very first miracle that God teaches Moses to perform is transforming his shepherd's staff into a snake. Moses runs to hide when he sees the snake; God coaxes him to pick it up by the tail and so turn it again into a staff. Moses's struggle to handle this snake, this masculine potency, like his uncircumcised lips, distances his authority from the authority automatically conveyed by patriarchy, the authority received from a father and passed down to a son. Moses is the recipient of a patrimony, part of a covenant made by God with his father and his father's father and generations before, but Moses is also outside of that lineage, raised by Egyptians and living among Midianites. His authority comes from God, not the world. God tells Moses to tell Pharaoh that "Israel is my firstborn son" (4:22)—it is God who takes the place of worldly authorities, who takes the place of all fathers, who challenges social hierarchies encrusted by tradition.

Moses's ability to turn his staff into a snake, mediated by Aaron (who performs the miracle), is ultimately not persuasive to Pharaoh. The Egyptian leader simply summons his own magicians and demonstrates that they, too, can turn a staff into a snake. This is the first of several moments where the Exodus narrative teaches us to perceive the difference between charisma and its simulacra. Pharaoh's magicians (the text includes with magicians "wise men," suggesting collective wisdom, the wisdom of tradition) might look in some ways precisely like Moses and Aaron as they work miracles, but Pharaoh's magicians use their seemingly extraordinary gifts to secure the powers that be, to maintain social hierarchy—to exult Pharaoh. Later in the narrative, famously, the Israelites grow restless as Moses is on Mount Sinai for forty days communing with God. The people have been told to worship their God, but mediation is absent and God is distant. They go astray. With Aaron's blessing, the people collect gold jewelry and melt it into a golden calf, which they worship—a deity that they can access directly, without mediation. In this case, the powers that be are more crudely material: gold, wealth, capital become the object of worship in place of God. The worship of the golden calf does resemble in many ways the worship of God, with rituals and sacrifices and songs, but it is decisively different. The golden calf—significantly, an object, not a person—does have a type of charisma, drawing the Israelites in, fulfilling their desire with its shine. The golden calf and Pharaoh's magicians represent authoritarian charisma, opposed to Moses's democratic charisma. They give viewers what the viewers want to see instead of inviting viewers to interrogate their own desires. Authoritarian charisma does not invite its audience to see themselves and their worlds in new ways. It awes, but at the end of the day it does not change: the rich and powerful become richer and more powerful.

Ridding the world of authoritarian charisma is a painful and bloody process. When Moses returns from Mount Sinai and sees that a festival is being celebrated in honor of the golden calf, he gathers the Israelites who remain loyal to him. He tells them, "Go back and forth from gate to gate throughout the camp, and each of you kill your brother, your friend, and your neighbor." To be rid of idols does not simply mean breaking them or tossing them into the sea. If the hold of an idol, if the hold of authoritarian charisma, is strong enough, it may be necessary for a community to be purged. This is less tragic than it may seem for the human has already been all but stamped out in those who worship an idol. They have entirely forgotten who they are, entirely embraced the description of what they are offered by those around them and the superficial desires that come along.

The first time God communicates with Moses, when he is in Midian, God appears not directly but through the intermediary of an angel, and that angel through the intermediary of a burning bush. It is essential that distance be maintained: "Come no closer," Moses is told, and Moses hides his face (3:5). When Moses protests that he cannot speak well, God suggests Aaron as an intermediary: "He indeed shall speak for you to the people; he shall serve as a mouth for you, and you shall serve as God for him" (4:16). But it is actually not the people to whom Aaron speaks. He speaks to the elders, and it is only they who pass on the message that God told to Moses to the people. Further, it is not just words that are mediated. While Hollywood depicts Moses as a miracle worker, impressing Pharaoh and the Jews, it is actually Aaron who performs miracles in public, using what he has been taught by Moses, who was in turn instructed by God. Even in earlier generations, God did not make Godself "fully known" to Abraham, Isaac, and Jacob. Who God is exceeds that, exceeds the God who is represented by tradition. When God finally decides to appear to the Israelites as they wander through the desert, God's appearance is enormously mediated. God orders (Moses to order the elders to order the people) that the Israelites are to stay away from Mount Sinai, on punishment of death. In addition to not climbing the mountain, they are to abstain from sexual relations, leaving God alone in the phallic position. There is thunder and lightning. There is smoke on the mountain, signaling the fire where God will appear—but the fire itself is not visible from the bottom of the mountain where the Israelites are. When God finally appears to Moses, God warns Moses that no one can see God's face; God covers Moses's eyes with God's hand. It is only after God has passed, as God is leaving, that Moses is able to see God's back. After this experience, a bit of the divine passes from God to Moses. The Israelite leader's face becomes radiant, so bright that it blinds those who see him, so bright that Moses needs to wear a veil if he is to be seen by others. Charisma, represented by radiance, is contagious: it passes, indirectly, from God to Moses and from Moses to the Israelites close to him: Aaron, Joshua, and others.

First among the laws that God decrees, the First Commandment, would seem to be a rejection of mediation. To condemn the worship of idols would seem to be an assertion of the direct relationship with God, unmediated by God's representatives. But in fact God at the same time presents a whole raft of intermediaries, of ways that God should be worshiped in God's absence (tabernacle specifications, proper vestments, and so on). God is concerned with proper mediation, not with pure presence. Idols of silver and gold represent faulty mediation, mediation that captures the gaze and superficially sates desire, not mediation that allows for critical examination of self and world. Similarly, God specifically warns against worshiping the gods of other people among whom the Israelites might live, such as the Egyptians. This might sound like jealousy, and it is sometimes represented as jealousy, but when God is understood negatively, as exceeding representation, the worship of foreign gods would simply mean the worship of gods that can be named, gods that can be described. These gods will tempt when the majority of a community embraces them. "You shall not follow a majority in wrongdoing," God decrees (23:2). Faith in God means a commitment that may run counter to the ways of the world. God's justice treats the individual, who they are, not what they are, not based on their social location. It is not the will of the majority. It is treatment of the other as one who images God. To Moses, God decrees, "You shall not pervert the justice due to your poor in their lawsuits," but God also decrees that the Israelites not "be partial to the poor in a lawsuit" (23:6; 23:3). Before God's law, each has equal dignity.

As the newly freed Israelites wander through the desert, Moses serves as their judge, resolving disputes by interpreting God's will. Moses's father-in-law, Jethro, a Medianite rather than an Israelite, visits and suggests that Moses should delegate to reduce his growing workload. Moses takes Jethro's advice exactly, choosing "able men" as officials who will resolve disputes over subcommunities of Israelites. If any dispute is too difficult, it will be referred to Moses. In other words, Moses establishes the beginnings of a legal system and appoints bureaucrats to enforce it—notably without divine inspiration, with the inspiration of a foreigner. Law is secular at first, but not for long. Shortly after Jethro's visit, the God of the Israelites codifies law for the community, handing it down to Moses on Mount Sinai. Yet the Exodus narrative makes it clear that Moses did not bring the law to a lawless community. Before Egypt, while they were in Egypt, and as they began wandering in the desert, the Israelites were to follow God's decrees, and they were aware of these decrees. First motivated by Jethro, then by God, Moses codified and systematized these decrees. Unlike the classic image of a charismatic lawgiver who overturns and re-creates law, Moses was accountable to a law that existed before him and that was not of his making. Even the laws proclaimed by God were not primarily laws as we traditionally understand them, or as Cecil B. DeMille would have us understand them. The vast majority have to do with codifying social norms and ritual practices: four sheep must be paid by a sheep thief if a sheep is stolen, foreigners are not to be mistreated, land is to lay fallow every seventh year, festivals should be celebrated honoring God three times a year, a lampstand of pure gold should be made with images of buds and blossoms and six branches for ritual purposes, and so on. Moses is not opposed to the law, but he is not the author of the law either. Law and tradition are difficult to disentangle; Moses stands at a moment when tradition and law intersect. Indeed, Moses may be seen as holding together tradition and law—which is to say, he may be seen as exemplifying authoritarian charisma. That tradition and law are compatible, that secular and worldly courts are compatible, is made possible by (a story of) a charismatic leader who unites the two in his self, extraordinarily gifted by God. This points to the fundamental ambiguity of Exodus, or rather, it points to the precariousness that always characterizes democratic charisma. The display of the human can short-circuit long-established social hierarchies, but it can also be swept up into the realm of mediation—recorded in sacred text, represented in film—and so confirm those social hierarchies.

Because of the obvious charisma of Charlton Heston, and because of the identification of Charlton Heston with Moses, it is tempting to imagine that Moses is at the root of scholarly discussions of charisma. He is not. Indeed, John Potts's *A History of Charisma* resists labeling anything before the time of Jesus charisma. The Israelite prophets only have "proto-charisma," on his account, and Moses receives no mention as an exemplary figure in charisma's history. The current, nonscholarly use of charisma at least in part grows out of the word's revivification by Max Weber in the early twentieth century. For Weber, charisma means "certain qualities of an individual personality by virtue of which he is considered extraordinary and treated as endowed with supernatural, superhuman, or at least specifically exceptional powers or qualities. These are such as are not accessible to the ordinary person, but are regarded as of divine origin or as exemplary" (*Economy and Society*, 241). Weber is particularly interested in charisma as a form of authority, distinct from traditional authority (following norms because they have been followed since time immemorial) and from legal-rational authority (following norms because they are codified and enforced by bureaucrats). When there is charismatic authority, norms are followed because they are proclaimed by an individual with extraordinary qualities, with divine gifts. Charismatic authority can disrupt old habits and hierarchies and create new ones, dependent on the words of the charismatic leader. For Weber, once a charismatic leader dies, his or her authority is usually formalized in rules (becoming legal-rational authority) or passed down to her children (becoming traditional authority). Moses of the popular imagination would seem to be a perfect example of charisma, on Weber's account, and as an accomplished scholar of Judaism Weber would certainly have been familiar with the Exodus narrative, but Weber does not use Moses as an example of charisma. Weber does generally refer to the office of the prophet as one that involves charisma, but his main models are more contemporary. When Weber does mention Moses, he is portrayed as a lawgiver and a politically shrewd unifier of the Israelites. The man who first inspired Weber to theorize charisma was not Moses but the poet and aesthete Stefan George. Indeed, Weber did not theorize charisma until 1910, after he had published *The Protestant Ethic and the Spirit of Capitalism*, and after his declining health had led him to leave his academic post. George, a flamboyant homosexual, had cultivated a circle of admirers in Heidelberg, and Weber, also in Heidelberg, was attempting to do the same. Weber was successful: his intellectual power and wide learning became legendary at the university even after he was long gone from teaching, and his legend would spread internationally as the century wore on. In short, Weber's interest began on a quite small scale, and it began with charisma tied to intellect and art.

Why does Weber avoid Moses? Perhaps because the Exodus narrative complicates the distinctions he has drawn between charismatic, traditional, and legal-rational authority. Specifically, the Exodus narrative shows how charisma is always intertwined with traditional and legal-rational authority because tradition and law are forms of mediation and charisma depends on mediation. Tradition provides us with the words, images, and performances that allow us to see, and so act in, our world. Those words, images, and performances are not invented by us or by our contemporaries. They have come down through the generations, and we cannot escape them if we wish to communicate, or even merely to live. Law, both formally codified and informal social norms, creates our normative universe. We do not just live in the world; our lives are always lived in relation to what law in this broad sense says we ought or ought not to do, what we ought or ought not to say. We cannot speak without the rules of grammar, without the rules of proper usage, and we cannot act without knowing how those in our position are expected to act. Moses is embedded in tradition, the tradition of his father and of his father's father, back to Abraham. He also codifies the law for his community in a broad sense: not just the Ten Commandments but a whole array of social norms, including dietary restrictions, holiday rituals, and acceptable clothing.

Moses does more than this. He encounters God, and he performs his humanity. This humanity is part of a web of mediation, from burning bushes and angels to Aaron and the Israelite elders, from tradition to law, but this humanity also exceeds mediation, just as God exceeds any name attributed to God. Moses's uncircumcised lips mark that humanity: they mark him as fleshy, imperfect, and ultimately quite ordinary. But humanity is more than physical description. The juxtaposition of ordinary and extraordinary performs the human by interweaving material and transcendent realities in a way that points beyond both. Moses is charismatic insofar as he is able to perform this excess, interrupting the web of mediation with the human who he is, and calling others to do the same, just as Moses was called by God. The result is a movement toward justice. The Israelites realize that they are not reducible to the world's description of them, to the Egyptians' description of them as slaves. As they realize that they are each human, their humanity resonates, catalyzed by charisma, and manifests in the movement across the sea, toward justice.

Weber did draw on the work of contemporary theologians who had begun exploring the importance of charisma in the New Testament and in the Christian tradition. These theologians argued that early Christian communities were held together not by rules but by the visible gifts of God announced in the book of Acts. As Paul writes in the first book of Corinthians, pagans were "led astray to idols that could not speak." Paul proclaims the true gifts of God, from the Spirit, offered "for the common good": wisdom, knowledge, faith, healing powers, miracle-working, prophecy, speaking in tongues, and the ability to interpret speech in tongues (1 Corinthians 12). It is such gifts, and reflection on their import, that form a theological account of charisma preceding Weber's sociological account, and this theological sense of charisma lives today alongside Weber's. Such divine gifts, charismata, are often at the center of movements for Christian renewal, such as the Second Great Awakening in early-nineteenth-century America or the more recent rise of global Pentecostalism. Charisma, on this Christian view, is not a quality of worldly elites. God offers different gifts to different people, and these gifts should be developed and revered. Charisma is democratic: extraordinary gifts are found in ordinary people. And charisma is contagious: it is capable of passing from one Christian to the next. Weber may have seen this model of charisma starkly opposed to the haughty charisma of the Hebrew prophets, and of Moses, speaking from on high in the name of God. But, in fact, as we saw from engaging with the Exodus text itself, the charisma of Moses is rather more complicated—rather more democratic.

One pressing question remains regarding the charisma of Moses, a question posed by Edward Said in an impassioned response to Michael Walzer. Walzer proposes reading Moses as a democratic figure, specifically as an advocate of social democracy in a way that navigates safely between the dangers of liberalism and Leninism. Walzer's Moses organizes the Israelites to take collective action against injustice. This Moses does not have a specific goal in mind, and he does not have an entire plan worked out, but he knows injustice when he sees it, and he knows how to organize people against it. What is essential about the Exodus story, on Walzer's account, is the movement toward justice, the faith that a better world is possible, and the willingness to put in hard work and endure suffering and delay in search of that better world. Said points out, rightly, that Walzer's Exodus story may be deeply concerned with the injustice suffered by the Israelites, but it is not particularly concerned with the injustice suffered by the Canaanites, whose land the Israelites are to occupy. The land of milk and honey that the Israelites are promised is inhabited; it is someone else's milk and honey that they will enjoy. If Exodus is to offer a model of justice, it would seem to be a model that is fundamentally flawed, producing as much injustice as it alleviates, if not more.

Said's worries about the Exodus narrative are certainly warranted, but the narrative is also inescapable. It is deeply woven into various traditions, not only the American (which is similarly invested in settler colonialism) but also the African American, to take but two examples. If we read Exodus as a story about nation-building, it is indeed problematic. If we read it as a story about the human, about uncovering the human beneath worldly misrepresentations of humanity, it holds promise. When Moses is depicted as having authoritarian charisma, when he is identified with Charlton Heston, he is the champion of a nation. When Moses is depicted with uncircumcised lips, performing democratic charisma, as he is depicted in the Hebrew Bible, Moses displays the human and calls us to do the same. This is not a decline from social justice to individual virtue. It is a call for social justice that begins with the critique of ideology, a challenge to the ways the world has us see ourselves and our surroundings. This is a shared enterprise—democratic charisma is contagious—and it can ignite a social movement. But democratic charisma is also precarious: it can quickly become authoritarian, quickly harden tradition and legality, amplifying rather than challenging injustice.

2

THE VIRTUE OF CHARISMA

What if charisma, instead of mysteriously arriving from the heavens, instead of being present in some and absent in others, is an essential component of our humanity—even *the* essence of our humanity? In theological terms, this is not so surprising: humans are created in the image of God, and human life is a gift from God. Some have special gifts as well, gifts of the Spirit, but all have this basic gift of life. Does this have any meaning outside a theological context? Does it have any meaning in an age when we look with suspicion on appeals to the otherworldly?

Philip Rieff compellingly argues that charisma is better understood as involving a certain inwardness than as involving divine gift. What this means is that charisma marks opacity. It marks something beyond what any list of external features— physical attributes, histories, relationships—could enumerate. What exactly is beyond these external features of a human being? The temptation to offer specific answers is a temptation to misunderstand the question. To name this excess, this inwardness, is to negate its status as inwardness. Judith Butler captures this quite precisely: "For representation to convey the human, then, representation must not only fail, but it must *show* its failure. There is something unrepresentable that we neverthe-less seek to represent, and that paradox must be retained in the representation we give" (*Precarious Life*, 144). Butler is saying that the human always involves something that cannot be rep-resented. The best way to represent it, the best way to name inwardness, is to dramatize the failure of all possible represen-tations, of all possible labels. Returning to a theological idiom: if the human being is created in the image of God, and if no human language is able to speak rightly about God, then there is part of the human being about which no human language can speak rightly.

Charisma, then, dramatizes inwardness. Charisma draws attention to the failure of any language to represent the human. In other words, rather than a gift from outside of the world, charisma marks an immanent break. It marks a point in the world itself that is essentially opaque—and so reminds us that we ourselves are essentially opaque. Charisma takes place in rela-tionships: those who observe charisma are not detached specta-tors but are themselves affected. The way they are affected is by recognizing the inadequacy of representation, that is, by real-izing that the way they understand the world does not quite work, and further that no attempt to fully grasp the world will quite work. Witnesses see how the charismatic figure does not match expectations, thwarting the mechanics of concepts and intuitions and so soliciting reflection by the witness on herself, on how she also is more than the world thinks she is, how she cannot even understand herself. Inwardness is contagious and charisma is the pathogen.

What does all this mean concretely? When we watch and listen to a charismatic figure, what we observe thwarts our ex-pectations. We are used to seeing and hearing all sorts of peo-ple, processing what they say, and reacting. Something goes wrong when we encounter a charismatic person. Her presentation is in many ways familiar but also in crucial ways unfamiliar. As our expectations are thwarted, at first the charismatic figure does not seem human. We know what humans are like, and this person is different. But as we look and listen further, we conclude that the charismatic figure is actually showing humanity at its purest. We realize that it is we who have been confused, it is we who, with hubristic confidence, believed we knew how to divide up the world into *these* people and *those*, many times over. And as we watch and listen further, we realize that this conclusion applies to ourselves. We must discern the ways that we have too easily understood ourselves, and the ways that we have too easily deferred to social norms without interrogating them.

Given this understanding, we can conclude that many times the word *charisma* is applied, it is not referring to charisma properly understood. Indeed, many times that the word *charisma* is used it refers to precisely the opposite of charisma as defined here. Such apparent charisma makes us think we are a certain sort of person we are not or otherwise confirms the mistaken ways we view the world. Let us call charisma that reveals our humanity *democratic charisma*, charisma that conceals our humanity *authoritarian charisma*. The label *democratic* points to the way in which charisma is not a property of an exclusive group of elites. It is a characteristic of all, more or less evident, capable of being developed (as books on how to become a charismatic business leader promise). This account of charisma is also democratic in that it embraces the power of the people, understood as a collection of ultimately unrepresentable individuals. Democratic charisma challenges those ideas and practices that would diminish or desecrate our humanity by equipping those who come in contact with charisma to critically evaluate the ideological and institutional mechanisms that tell us who we are supposed to be and how the world is supposed to run. Authoritarian charisma, in contrast, sanctifies just those mechanisms. It mutes critical capacities and defers to an authority to provide direction. That specific authority stands in for all authority: for the powers that be.

This distinction between democratic and authoritarian charisma seems more straightforward than it is. For example, all forms of charisma would seem to cultivate habits of deference that are more authoritarian than democratic. But when we consider democratic charisma we must also alter our sense of scale. Instead of thinking of the actor on thousands of big screens or the politician speaking to hundreds, why not think about the charismatic member of the neighborhood association, school board, or soup kitchen? The larger the platform, the more difficult it is to witness inwardness. It is not impossible, but the ease with which inwardness is transformed into familiar cultural tropes, familiar styles of performance, increases along with the degree of mediation. Charisma that is democratic on a small scale can quickly become authoritarian as it is caught up in layers of representation. To pierce through those layers, displaying inwardness that is not easily assimilable to a familiar form, requires careful perceptiveness and responsiveness. However, this challenge of scale should not be overemphasized. All democratic charisma, even on a very small scale, faces dramatic challenges. After all, we are told who we are over and over and over, year after year, by others and by ourselves. We are immersed in a world of representation and mediation that is enormously expansive and resilient: this is how we navigate the world, individually and collectively. These layers of representation and mediation have sedimented over the centuries, forming the substance of our culture. To scrape through these layers of sediment and show their inadequacy, to show that we are different than who we say we are and who we have been told we are, is a tremendous feat at any scale.

How is such a feat accomplished? Not with a divine gift, but through the cultivation of virtue. Nothing is needed from outside the world, or even from outside the self. What makes us human is the fact that the world's representations of us are inadequate. The challenge is to articulate that inadequacy in an idiom that is not overdetermined by the world, and so betrays its purpose. Everyone has the capacity to articulate this inadequacy, if only in a stutter, or silence. After all, it is just as if the world's representations of us are our own; if this artificiality were imperceptible, then those representations would be fully constitutive of us. This disjunction between what we are, in the world's representations, and who we are, exceeding those representations, can be communicated more or less effectively. It requires a nuanced awareness of how one is perceived and an ability to toggle one's self-representation in a way that both acknowledges that perception and troubles it. This might be crudely described as self-awareness, but that does not quite convey the agency involved. Charisma requires not only knowing how one is perceived, including by one's self, but also an ability and willingness to manipulate that perception. This manipulation cannot be aimed at advancing self-interest or the interests of others because those interests already take for granted given modes of perception. Self-interest is based on an understanding of the self that has been given by the world just as the interests of others depend on how the world perceives them. Rather than being motivated by interest, charisma is motivated by that which animates all virtue: a desire for something beyond what is offered by the world.

Virtues are dispositions. They are tendencies to act in certain ways in certain circumstances. The Aristotelian conception of virtue has attracted the attention of many scholars in recent years, with its emphasis on virtue as a mean between extremes and on virtue as cultivated in community. On this view, virtue is of the world, not beyond the world or despite the world. If this were so, the virtuous person would be the least charismatic, for she or he would be fully, perfectly formed by her community, with no excess—not too much of this sort of action, not too little of that sort of action. In contrast, the Socratic and Christian conceptions of virtue begin with the intuition that the customs of the communities in which we live are deeply flawed. These customs require sustained interrogation from the perspective not of moderation but of truth. The virtuous person is the good person, the person who is disposed to act in ways that are truly good, not in ways that seem to be good. To do this requires sustained reflection and criticism. This may happen collectively, with others who share a commitment to truth (Socrates and his interlocutors, Church), but it is not reducible to the views or interests of that collectivity. Such reflection and criticism cannot remain at the level of the abstract. It is not an intellectual exercise disconnected from practice, from life. This sustained reflection and criticism animate virtue: they mold the dispositions away from the socially acceptable and toward the truthful. In both the Socratic and the Christian traditions, it is clearly understood that in this world there is no access to the absolute. Our lives will never be fully virtuous; virtue is a question of more or less. But there is also a sense that virtue brings reward: happiness deeper and more sustaining than the superficial pleasures offered by worldly goods.

Charisma is not a specific virtue in the way that patience or temperance or perseverance, each important to the Aristotelian tradition, are specific virtues. In the Socratic and Christian traditions, these may indeed be virtuous, but they are virtuous to the extent that they are animated by a desire for the good beyond the world. When we are disposed to act in ways that set aside worldly prerogatives, that set aside the way the world would have us perceive it, we appear charismatic. The observer sees in us something unexpected, something that cannot be classified in familiar terms. This is our humanity, the human in us. It is our capacity to act as more than machines that pursue quantifiable interests in rational ways. On the one hand, charisma would seem to require an extremely subtle understanding of the workings of representation and mediation in order to thwart the all-too-common, all-too-easy ways charisma can be ignored or reduced. On the other hand, when it is understood as a Socratic virtue, charisma seems easy. The mechanisms of representation and mediation are automatically short-circuited when confronting a human being manifesting her humanity— no effort is necessary. By definition, that humanity cannot be represented; indeed, that which cannot be represented in us is the human. To manifest one's humanity means to quest for that place where representation fails, to seek out the limitations of the world's ways of seeing itself, to seek truth beyond the world, which is to say, to pursue virtue in the Socratic sense.

Democratic charisma is virtuous; authoritarian charisma is vicious. Authoritarian charisma appears to transcend the world but actually embodies the world, strengthening the hold that the ways of the world have on us and strengthening the social hierarchies that they reinforce. Consider the figure of the community elder. This role itself, like that of the teacher or father, tends to bring with it charisma: people call the old wise man (or woman) charismatic. Why is this? On the one hand, there are certain cultural tropes of the charismatic that tend to be associated with the community elder: speaking slowly and apparently thoughtfully, having broad knowledge but also a sense of humility, being treated with deference, and so on. Because someone shares features with those who are taken as charismatic, she too is treated as charismatic. But such resemblances do not get to the heart of the matter. The community elder is seen as personifying social norms. All of what one ought or ought not to do in the community is intuitively understood by the elder, so if a question of what to do arises, she is the one to whom the community turns. Even a new question, never dealt with before, can be directed to the elder so that the community can stay true to its values even as its world expands. This deep understanding of a community's normative world brings with it the appearance of charisma. Community members may be debating among themselves, each interpreting the community's norms differently based on his or her vantage point—young or old, worker or employer, marginal or central, bureaucrat or scofflaw. After consulting with the elder, they quickly understand and accept. They realize the specificity of their position, and they recognize in the words of the elder, who has played many roles in her long life, the familiar norms accepted broadly by the community. The elder's ability seems rather mystical when her explication of tradition prompts quick conversion, but it is more the warm reassurance of tradition that the elder conveys.

Such a description is, of course, an ideal type, but this community elder is a figure who is easily recognizable and who is just as present in our contemporary world as in the premodern. The news media enjoy describing "elder statesmen" who resolve intractable political disputes, but we have such figures among our neighbors and coworkers and family members as well. Their charisma seems inherently antidemocratic because it is not evenly distributed and it is not achieved through cultivation. It is an attribute of some because they have experienced much.

Importantly, the charisma of the community elder is achieved through the appearance of knowledge, not of ignorance. The elder may not know everything about the world, but she masterfully understands the values of her community and how they are to be applied. As she applies them, she brings her community together, allowing community members from disparate positions to recognize the values they have in common and to feel united as one. In other words, the community elder reaffirms the ways of the world, the ways we collectively see and act in the world. She challenges individuals who have strayed from the community's self-understanding because of their self-interest or their limited experience. To revere such figures as gifted by the gods, in the sense of wielding divinely sanctioned authority, is to understand charisma as authoritarian. It is to dangerously strengthen the normative force behind tradition. The reprimand for going astray, once a word of warning, becomes a threat of exile or extermination when community norms are understood as divinely sanctioned. This is the danger of authoritarian charisma.

Ideal types conceal real world complexity. While respected community elders may embody social norms and may personify tradition, they also often have an ironic distance from rules. Having lived to see many rules broken, many lives broken, and many lives transformed, the community elder avoids overinvestment in discerning the way things ought to be. She knows that things can be quite different than they are: they once were quite different and they certainly will be quite different again. Life goes on; despair is unnecessary. The advice of the elder is often opaque, requiring interpretation but also refusing investment in the present terms of debate. This is all the more clear in special, culturally specific types of community elder such as the oracle or the hermit. Rather than resolving community debate

with a definitive ruling, as a judge would, the elder offers an
occasion to step back from the terms of the debate and reconsider what it means to be engaged collectively in the debate,
ultimately in a conversation premised on shared values. In this
way it might seem as though the community elder actually represents an example of democratic charisma. She refuses to accept the way the world sees itself, and she refuses the role of
judge when it is asked of her. The community elder certainly
has the potential to possess democratic charisma, just as everyone does. Yet the role of community elder (or oracle or hermit)
usually overdetermines her charisma, turning it authoritarian.
Charisma does not exist in a vacuum. It exists in relationship to
how one is perceived by others, which means in relationship
with the modes of representation and mediation that govern
how we perceive. Democratic charisma short-circuits representation and mediation; authoritarian charisma derives its power
from representation and mediation. After having taken the
long hike up the mountain to receive advice from the hermit,
having heard your whole life what a wise old man he is, having
resolved to follow whatever words of wisdom he dispenses,
there is very little that the hermit can do to break free of the
role into which he has been cast. Whatever he says or does not
say will be heard as serious explications of community values,
and those values will now receive something like divine sanc-
tion. They have been spoken from on high, from the lips of the
divinely gifted sage. Existing forms of community, with all the
hierarchy and inequality that those entail, are reinforced: authoritarian charisma is inevitable.

There are exceptions, however. These exceptions are quintessentially democratic, arising from those whom we consider
more nearly equals rather than from those overdetermined by
their role as authorities. The grandmother or great-aunt or el-

derly neighbor or retired coworker: such individuals may possess the experiences of the community elder without being overdetermined by the role of community elder. This is not to say that all old people are charismatic and the ones who avoid renown have democratic charisma. Rather, it is to say that we all know someone who has democratic charisma. Such individuals have experienced much in their life: they have had turns of fortune, they have played different roles, and they have met different sorts of people. They do not take themselves too seriously, and they do not take the world too seriously. They say and do things that surprise us. They remind us that we should not judge others prematurely, that we should not accept the ways of seeing others to which we have become accustomed—and that we should not accept the ways of seeing ourselves to which we have become accustomed. There is no sense that the elder with democratic charisma distills all of the wisdom of a community. Elders know a few things that they have experienced, and they have some views about what is right and what is wrong. More significant than these, they are aware of the limits to their knowledge—they are familiar with both the known unknowns and the unknown unknowns—and they are aware of how we strive to grasp the world when at the same time the world is grasping us. And they are practiced at critical refusal, reminding us that whatever rewards the world promises if we allow ourselves to be grasped are less than the rewards of truth, goodness, and beauty displayed in a life that eludes the world's grasp.

While the community elder may be one of the most familiar figures of charisma, there is another such figure so familiar that it is easy to forget: the parent. While the figure of the father is often distant and wise, the figure of the mother is often overbearing and practical. These are, clearly, figures from the cultural imaginary, not real people, but it is the cultural imaginary that casts real people in roles that we can recognize. Beyond the cultural imaginary, it is clear that we have special relationships with our parents, and we see them as special people, if only for their sustained presence in our lives during our formative years. (The configuration of this presence certainly varies significantly across cultures and histories.) The young child looks at her parents with amazement and awe. They know so much, can do so many things, and can speak in mysterious ways. Like the community elder, the parent has a special relationship with normativity. The parent (for Freud, the father) is the first to say "no"—that is, the first to introduce the child to the normative world. Even when parents are not directly constructing the child's normative universe through praise and reprimand, parents occupy this role long enough that the child recognizes them as trusty authorities about what ought or ought not to be done in the world—just as elders and oracles are so recognized by adults. Moreover, the parent also contains mystery: the parents' knowledge and ability have no bounds from the child's perspective. Freud joins this mystery with normativity in the figure of the parent's penis (at first the child imagines both parents have them), which represents the mysterious power possessed by the parent in quantities enormously greater than it is by the child. Such power and mystery enchant, comfort, and haunt. No matter how the parent speaks, the parent's words have a power beyond their content or their tone: the parent possesses a seemingly effortless charisma.

Is the charisma of the parent authoritarian? It is certainly not democratic. The child has no illusion that she could possess the same mysterious power as the parent. Yet the parent's charisma does not quite seem authoritarian either. It is not so much that the texture of the normative world is reinforced and so made rigid by a divinely gifted figure. In a sense, the parent constitutes the normative world: without the father's initial "no," the world would not be filled with things one ought to do and things one ought not to do. For the young child, the parent is God, not gifted by God. There is no mediation, so there can be no charisma. Unlike the authoritarian charismatic figure, the parent does not need to mute the child's reason and manipulate her affect. The parent determines for the child what counts as a reason.

It may be imprecise to speak of charisma in relation to the small child, but what about as the child grows into an adult, capable of reasoning on her own, capable of engaging with the world on her own? As she grows, the child learns that the parents are not the ultimate source of normativity, that they are not the fount of all reason. Parents are among the many people with opinions, idiosyncrasies, limitations, and histories. Yet the relationship with the parents remains distinct; the parents' words continue to carry excess meaning. Despite extended intimate interaction, the parent always retains a touch of mystery, of unpredictability. The too-easy psychological explanation for Hitler, that he fills the role of father, is a claim about the primacy of the charisma of the parent. But such explanations overlook that an essential aspect of our relationship with our parents is our ability to relate to them when their stature has diminished from God to human, as it were. This is not a unique experience: it is the experience of becoming an adult, an experience shared by all. Indeed, it is the transition from authoritarian charisma to democratic charisma. Authoritarian charisma is both alluring and suspect because it models that charisma of the parent felt by the small child, that relationship with no mediation.

Mediation is essential to democratic charisma because it is essential to the world in which we live. The fantasy of absolute presence, of direct access to another person or to the world, is essentially undemocratic, essentially authoritarian. This is the fantasy of a return to childhood, to the mother's breast, to the womb—or to a god who speaks directly into your ear. When such images of intimacy are applied to the world in which we adult human beings live, we lose our sense of our own agency and responsibility. To say that in such circumstances we treat another as an authority would be misleading. Treating as an authority requires distance and decision. The fantasy of absolute presence does not help us in navigating our world; it constitutes our world. If God whispers in our ear that the world is flat, that humans do not cause climate change, or that Iraq possesses weapons of mass destruction, that is how the world is. Gods (or mothers) experienced with such intimacy do not tell us how to see the world; they make up our world. For us, their concepts must refer to realities, and we will necessarily witness the realities to which they refer. Such relationships can be authoritarian when the person with whom we are intimate embraces the norms of our community, as gods and mothers often do. They are relatively benign when we are young, still learning those norms. When we are older, these relationships—involving authoritarian charisma—can become problematic because, first, they sanctify and so overvalue a community's norms and because, second, they cultivate habits of deference that pacify community members. These two problems clearly compound: the more reverence is paid to a community's norms, the more pacific its members, and the more pacific its members, the more they are content to sanctify rather than interrogate its norms.

Parental relationships begin with minimal mediation, but soon we are immersed in a world requiring communication. To communicate is to communicate by means of something, for example, by means of words or gestures. For communication to succeed, these means must be shared by both parties. There must be a shared language or a shared set of images or a shared repertoire of performances. What is shared for communication to succeed mediates. It is an unavoidable accompaniment to every conversation, and to every relationship beyond the womb and the breast. It is not chosen by us, and we can do little to change it with the exception of a slight innovation here or there. To communicate with those who are more distant from us, who cannot directly hear our words, see our pictures, or witness our performances, we utilize the technologies of media to package and deliver what we have to say. We write letters, broadcast songs on the radio, or update our Facebook status. Media are also not created by us, and they are barely altered by us. Media are, indeed, also forms of mediation. They shape what can be communicated and how we relate to those with whom we communicate even though they would not seem to have agency in the communication.

Language, images, and performances feel warmer, more flexible, because we can imagine one of our ancestors having a novel experience and then suddenly inventing a word, drawing a picture, or performing a dance that relates to this experience—with myriad such experiences forming the substance of mediation. Mediation is cultural: it grows out of and deeply marks our collective identity as a community. While it might not be substantially affected by any one individual, it is substantially affected by the experiences of a community over time, over generations. In contrast, media seem cold, hard, and modern, created in the garage of Steve Jobs or the laboratory of Alexander Graham Bell. Media technologies seem orthogonal to the substance of culture, perhaps affecting it but rarely affected by it, rather like the weather or the mountains. Just as the relationship between humans and their environment is rather more complex than such images of exteriority would imply, so too is our relationship with media. Consider a speech delivered to the citizens of ancient Athens. While the ancient world would seem to be the last place you would find media technology, the speaker needs both mediation and something quite like media to be effective. Certainly she must know the appropriate language, metaphors, and gestures. But she must also know how to control her voice in a way that can reach a few thousand people; she must know what words and images will pull on the heartstrings of her listeners; she likely paid a professional sophist to draft a speech for her; and she must be cognizant of how reports of the speech are likely to circulate among those Athenians who did not attend her speech—and perhaps even among those peoples of different cultures living in different city-states with a stake in (or amused by) Athenian affairs. It is not just culturally determined styles of performance that are employed in such a setting. It is also something closer to contemporary mass media: manipulation of the voice (speakers were said to practice amplification by speaking with rocks in their mouths), an industry of writers, and an attentiveness to diverse direct and secondary audiences. To approach from the other direction: television, paradigmatic of modern mass media, relies heavily on culturally specific styles of performance that develop and transform within a generation. Thinking through mediation and media together reminds us of the technological aspects of mediation as well as the culturally constructed aspects of mass media. The desire to separate the two, to treat media as cold and abstract while mediation is relational and porous, perhaps is a product of the same desire that would have us overlook mediation altogether: the desire for absolute presence.

For many who attack charisma, it is precisely media that make charisma so dangerous. Seeing a larger-than-life charismatic performance on the movie screen or reading about the charisma of a distant leader in the newspaper is a quite different experience than watching a charismatic colleague circulate at a reception or hearing a charismatic candidate for city council at a town meeting. Without media amplification, a speaker's apparent gifts would always seem to be brought back to earth by her humanity. No matter how great the rhetorical heights of the speaker, when you can notice the missing button from her shirt, the slight smell from under her arms, or the strand of hair just a tad askew, it is difficult to be entirely enchanted by her performance. Magnified and circulated, a man becomes a myth, a larger-than-life figure of wonder—quite nearly a god. Even relatively primitive media technology seemingly has this effect: loudspeakers or even the "people's mic" used at Occupy Wall Street protests, with activists collectively repeating the words of the speaker to allow those words to ripple out through a crowd, make it harder to recognize the charismatic speaker as a fellow human being.

This distrust of media is misguided. In fact, it is acknowledgment of and critical engagement with media that make possible democratic charisma. Why this is becomes clear when we acknowledge the continuity between media and mediation, and the unavoidability of both. Critics of charisma are worried about media but embrace mediation because they are worried about the unmediated. Recognizing the entanglement of media and mediation makes such a critique untenable. What critics of charisma rightly object to is the airbrushing that media entail. In other words, the charismatic individual appears flawless, slick. This is, indeed, part of authoritarian charisma—but authoritarian charisma is not the only form of charisma. At its best, as democratic, charisma juxtaposes an ordinary, flawed individual with an extraordinary performance. Charisma comes about because of this dissonance. If charisma at its best, as democratic charisma, performs the failure of representation, the dissonance between clearly imperfect performer and nearly perfect performance is one way to do this. Our expectations are thwarted: what we see is not what we get. Socrates was ugly. Moses stuttered. Martin Luther King, Jr., and Winston Churchill were short. When celebrity and charisma are conflated, when it is media figures who become the paradigms of charisma, it is easy to forget that visual or aural reminders of imperfection were once essential to charisma—and so it becomes easy to believe that all charisma is authoritarian.

Even more significant than the imperfections of the charismatic figure is the way democratic charisma succeeds to the extent that the charismatic figure thwarts the expectations of her audience. If she did not, there would be no surprise, no mystery. Charisma would be the excellent rather than the extraordinary. Excellence suggests that there is an established cultural form that the performer has mastered: the excellent cellist, the excellent doctor, the excellent politician, the excellent public speaker. When the relevant cultural form depends on media, the lines between excellence and charisma begin to blur. The excellent film actor and the excellent talk radio host are often described as charismatic. This is a loose use of *charisma*, or, more precisely, the concept in play is authoritarian charisma. Excellence at a cultural form reinforces and reinvigorates the cultural form—and the culture as a whole, together with all of its hierarchies and inequalities. In contrast, the excellence of democratic charisma will likely remain contested because it relates uncomfortably to given cultural forms. The charismatic figure is not beyond or outside of a culture, but she recognizes that the role in which the culture wishes to cast her does not capture who she is. Her charisma comes about as she struggles to articulate this inadequacy. This means having an acute self-awareness of the role in which the charismatic figure is cast, of the way in which she is seen, and an equally acute awareness of the cultural conventions accompanying that role. To be charismatic in the democratic sense is to be excellent at standing inside and outside such a role at once, thereby encouraging one's audience to reflect on the contingency of that role and to reflect on the way that the humanity of the charismatic figure and the humanity of the viewer exceed the roles in which they are cast.

These roles are shaped by cultural forces outside of the control of the charismatic figure. They are shaped by that cultural substance that is sometimes called media, sometimes called mediation, but that includes both. Democratic charisma involves an intuitive awareness of the relevant parts of this cultural substance, whether it be the relevant words, the relevant images, the relevant styles of performance—or the relevant technologies and media conventions, the intonation of the podcaster as well as the right kind of microphone to make a podcast, for example. If there is not an awareness of this cultural substance—a term less familiar but more evocative than convention, for we do not usually describe performance repertoires as mere convention—then the only possibility for charisma is through excellence, meaning the only possibility for charisma is for authoritarian charisma. Of course awareness is not nearly enough: the charismatic figure agilely toys with this cultural substance in order to assert herself. In some ways this is more difficult when the cultural substance in question involves mass media. Idiosyncratic performance can quickly become convention. Every American public radio host now has the high-pitched quasi-stutters of Ira Glass. For charisma to remain democratic when it is broadcast widely and when it depends on flexible conventions and evolving technology requires extreme performative agility of the sort rarely seen. This problem is clearly compounded by the way that charisma itself has become conventional, grabbing hold of those who begin to express democratic charisma and casting them in the media-prescribed role of the charismatic figure, which is to say, degrading their democratic charisma into authoritarian charisma. For these reasons, democratic charisma is more often found on a smaller scale, where the forms of mediation in question respond more slowly to innovation and where pressure from followers, eager to impose their own conventional understandings onto the charismatic performer, is felt less strongly.

Just as important as mediation when we think about democratic charisma is representation. The fantasy of direct access to god or (m)other precludes representation: it is about what is present, not about what is represented. A similar fantasy shades how we understand charisma. Simply being in the presence of the charismatic figure, being touched by her, touching something that she touched, walking somewhere that she once walked, allows for at least the partial transmission of the gift held by the charismatic figure to her followers. If she says a word or makes a speech, all the better. In that case, what the word is, what it points to in the world, does not matter so much as its existence, its presence. To have touched the hem of Mother Teresa, shaken the hand of the university president, or taken a meeting with someone who once took a meeting with Bill Clinton is to have received a divine gift through what seems to be the transitive property of charisma. (Note, incidentally, that in this case the enthusiast of charisma embraces explicit mediation.) Such an understanding of charisma describes yet another variety of authoritarian charisma. It describes charisma without humanity, charisma that could equally be applied to an object or a place as it could be to a person. This wide application of charisma at first seems to further democratize it, to extend it beyond the human sphere to the domain of the nonhuman, an increasingly trendy domain in certain scholarly circles. In fact, this account of charisma is authoritarian. As charisma passes from one place to another, object to person or person to object, there is no mediation. Standing next to the silent guru, charisma is imagined to flow unimpeded in all directions; the culturally specific styles of performance that are always in play are ignored.

The charisma of the lover would also seem to be authoritarian, deriving from the fantasy of relation without mediation and spread over body parts, pieces of clothes, smells, and objects touched. It is clear that romantic love does involve something like charisma. We relate to our beloved in a qualitatively, not quantitatively, different way than we relate to everyone else. That difference is not reducible to a greater level of intimacy. The beloved entrances because of something she is supposed to possess. Her words and gestures always bring with them signs of this excess that captivates. The beloved does not attract a crowd, but this does not diminish the sense in the lover that she is witnessing something spectacular. All this, of course, is the myth of romantic love rather than its practice. To confuse reality and myth will inevitably lead to devastation as the flaws and earthy specificity of the beloved eventually pierce the inflated image that has been created. Such devastation is rare because it is generally understood (even if not stated explicitly) that mediation is essential to romantic love—and that mediation does not preclude the appearance of charisma. There are a bevy of stylized cultural performances and a technical vocabulary that are employed by the lovers: the first kiss as well as, later, the off-to-work kiss; the first date with its appropriate conversation topics, locales, and habiliments; the freighted question of time that elapses between communication in the early stages of court-ship; and much more. There are also the enforcers of cultural convention: family members, opinionated friends and cowork-ers, and the judgmental-seeming couple at the next table over in the restaurant. Media are essential: once the letter, then the phone, now the text. Yet despite all these forms of mediation, the notion persists that there is "the one" out there, that soul mates exist, that the next Tinder swipe could reveal Prince Charming.

In short, romantic love in practice involves both mediation and charisma—in other words, it involves democratic charisma. It is less that the beloved is divine than that she is fully human. We appreciate the human in her in a way that we appreciate no one else. Her humanity is continually unfolding as our expecta-tions are continually thwarted, as we are continually reminded that what makes her human is our failure to fully grasp with our tired concepts who she is. Recognizing the humanity of the beloved transforms us as well. It shakes us out of a rut, remind-ing us that before we thought we fully understood the world we were curious, and we ought to be curious again. Moreover, as we ourselves are loved, as our lover is continually surprised and intrigued by us, we are prompted to see ourselves differently. We were accustomed to seeing ourselves one way, to describing ourselves in that way, but in love we are seen otherwise and so we wonder whether we may, indeed, be otherwise. Experienc-ing such love, experiencing ourselves and our world anew, we have a certain radiance—a certain charisma. This charisma is essentially democratic because it takes aim at the calcified con-ventions of the world as it is and allows us to imagine other-wise. Even more, it allows us to model what it looks like to imagine otherwise to those who witness the charisma produced by love.

It is important to distinguish romantic love, a culturally and historically specific practice, from desire as such. Desire is also closely associated with charisma. Colloquially, the charismatic speaker might light on fire the hearts of her listeners. The nineteenth-century speaker advancing abolitionism or the temperance movement, or belief in Jesus Christ, aimed at cultivating listeners' desire and aimed to direct them toward a particular plan of action in the world or in the auditor's own life. Critics of charisma are suspicious of such desire. It would seem to override reason. Rather than explaining why one ought to abolish slavery, prohibit alcohol, or surrender one's life to Jesus Christ, the speaker riles up the audience with a mix of images and anecdotes that never add up to an argument. The results may be laudatory, but the process is deficient and unsustainable—rather like the increased altruism of those who have just smelled fresh bread or just been surprised with good news.

Here again the distinction between democratic and authoritarian charisma is useful. The effect of both types of charisma is to be entranced, but authoritarian charisma numbs while democratic charisma engages. In the former, the charismatic figure fulfills desires that the witness already had, for example, for a certain conventional type of physical beauty. The desires fulfilled in this way are insatiable: the more they are fulfilled, the more desire they elicit. We want to see the movie over and over again, and we cannot wait until the next Cary Grant or Jimmy Stewart film is released. In contrast, democratic charisma does not fulfill existing desires with the object an audience seems to covet. The observer keeps returning to the figure of democratic charisma because this figure keeps satisfying a desire the witness did not know she had, and the charismatic figure keeps provoking new desires with little relationship to the observer's old desires. A nationalist demagogue fuels the preexisting nationalist passions of her listeners whereas a charismatic prison abolitionist, for example, contests the way the world is represented (that prisons are natural and necessary) and creates a new, unprecedented desire in her audience (to abolish prisons). In the case of authoritarian charisma, reason is muted by the compounding force of desire; reason can only offer friction to such increase. In the case of democratic charisma, the novelty encountered requires engagement with both reason and desire. What is this I am hearing about? It is not something I am familiar with—is she trying to say that it is like *this* or *that* which I am familiar with? How does it differ from them? How can I make sense of my novel, nascent passion given my other commitments? Whenever we venture into the unknown, even when fueled by powerful desire, we must orient ourselves. This orientation requires reason not as friction slowing the growth of our passion but as part of how the passion itself is constituted.

Put another way, authoritarian charisma draws us outside of the conceptual domain whereas democratic charisma depends on the conceptual. This is simply an extension of the different relations to mediation in these two types of charisma. Concepts are a basic form of mediation, even more basic than language. As we engage with the world, we locate our experiences on the map of concepts that is available to us; equally, we begin with this conceptual map to orient our engagement with the world. There are times when we set it aside: this is the goal of many forms of meditation, for example, and it is also described by artists and athletes who are so in "the moment" during a performance that conceptual thought would make them stumble. This is also the experience of authoritarian charisma. One who possesses authoritarian charisma so entrances the observer that all thoughts are pushed out of her head and only the image of the charismatic figure remains, an idol. In contrast, democratic charisma is defined by the fact that it short-circuits the way we represent the world. Such a charismatic individual herself is always different than she seems, more than meets the eye, and the effect of the encounter with the charismatic individual is to realize that there is more to the world, as well, than meets the eye. This challenge to what meets the eye, to our conventional ways of seeing the world, is a challenge to our concepts. It is a reminder that they do not perfectly map onto the world. As we witness the charismatic figure, we attempt to place her within our map of concepts, but each attempt fails. Similarly, that of which she speaks or that performance she offers thwarts our expectations. Democratic charisma leverages our desire for the world to make sense, for a healthy play of intuitions and concepts that allows us to navigate our worlds. In other words, the desire at work in democratic charisma is desire to understand our world and ourselves, desire to make sense of the limitations of the way the world would have us see it, and would have us see ourselves. The desire involved in democratic charisma is quintessentially Socratic: the desire to know oneself, and to know as such, a desire that means a critical engagement with how we are told the world is. Like Socrates, figures of democratic charisma solicit the use of long-dormant reason to explore how the concepts through which we view the world are inadequate. The more inadequate they are, the more we desire to understand, to probe further.

In short, authoritarian charisma generates followers, awaiting more and more fulfillment from the charismatic leader; democratic charisma is contagious, creating more and more charismatic individuals, individuals who understand that they are not who they have been represented to be. One thinks, for example, of the final protest in which Martin Luther King, Jr., participated, where the striking public employees wore sandwich

boards proclaiming, "I am a MAN." The striking workers notably do not give this proclamation any content. They do not explain what it means to be a man, but they claim, indeed perform, that they are something they have been told they are not.
The world, particularly the wealthy and powerful whose interests the dominant ideas of the world advance, denies the humanity of the striking workers, and they respond exclusively in the
negative: the world is wrong. Here is evidence of the contagion
of democratic charisma. There is no need to argue that the
workers designed these signs immediately after hearing King
speak. Rather, it is the interrogation of world and self that he
provoked that resonated far and near. In Memphis and before,
King refused to sate the desires of his listeners and instead
prompted them to see the world differently, to desire a different
world. (King's case is more complex, as will be discussed in
chapter 4.) It is too simplistic to say that democratic charisma
prompts action while authoritarian charisma leads to compla-
cency. Rather, democratic charisma stimulates reflection, individual and collective, without providing answers—while
discouraging answers. Those Memphis sanitation workers did
not need to be told that they were men, by King or by anyone
else. They knew it already, felt it, but rarely articulated it. Democratic charisma stimulates, rather than teaches, critical reflection.
It stokes the characteristically human capacities to reason and
desire, and it offers an occasion for their collective practice.

Some political theorists, most notably Jeffrey Green, have
recently and forcefully argued that it is the role of the spectator
that is essential to democracy, not the role of the political actor.
In some ways this point is so obvious that it only needs saying
to those who are caught in a spider web of abstraction. The way
that the vast majority of people today, and probably in most
places and at most times, participate in politics is to watch. They

watch television commercials and debates, they occasionally watch speeches or hearings. They are not passive observers. They make judgments using reason and emotion. They talk to friends, family, neighbors, and coworkers about the politics they see or that they read about. They comment on blogs, yell at their television, or ask a critical question. Rarely do they take part in a protest, volunteer for a campaign, lobby their representatives, or run for office themselves. From this perspective, political virtues are virtues of the spectator: attentiveness to the honesty conveyed by a speech or debate performance, judgment about the soundness of arguments and the persuasiveness of appeals, and assessment of leadership ability based on media-staged performances. When democracy is said to be government of the people, by the people, what the people here means is the collective of those who watch. When there is nothing to watch, there is no democracy. When those who watch are poor viewers, lacking in perceptiveness and judgment, democracy is weak; when those who watch are good spectators, democracy is strong. When the formal political involvement of the vast majority of people is limited to voting, with a choice between two candidates, democracy is not dead; indeed, an election prompts vigorous practices of spectatorship and so may represent democracy at its strongest.

This view of contemporary democracy is quite compelling, but it does seem rather undemocratic. While spectators have the ability to vote, they do not have the ability to choose the candidates or the issues that are on the table. Given the size of contemporary polities, media necessarily play a huge, unchecked role in determining what spectators will be able to watch. The people, understood as spectators, are so demobilized that they must depend on the goodwill of elites to maintain regular elections. Finally, and crucially, this emphasis on spectatorship as essential to democracy overlooks the nuances of charisma even though it is deeply dependent on charisma.

The intuition that gives rise to the scholarly interest in democratic spectatorship is that charismatic performance need not be authoritarian. Spectators can respond to charismatic figures critically; they need not be enchanted. A charismatic performance can in fact occasion critical engagement, careful thought about aspects of the world that were otherwise ignored or taken for granted. This may be the case, but it is not the case for all charisma. There is, indeed, charisma that blinds and distracts, charisma that fulfills and encourages preexisting desires, charisma that reaffirms social hierarchies and inequities. It is not clear whether, during a Fox News–produced US presidential debate, for example, it is possible for democratic charisma to stand alongside authoritarian charisma. When the repertoire of legible performances is so circumscribed, the spectator's judgment is most likely to be a judgment of how well a pregiven role was performed by the politician. Even if it were possible for the spectator to judge something like integrity, the meaning of integrity would be with respect to the expected role. It would mean consistently acting as one is expected to act. This is quite different from acting how one ought to act.

Most troubling about the account of democratic citizen as spectator is how it strips away the rich, varied connotations of democracy so that democracy comes to mean responsiveness to a narrow sphere of political elites. If authoritarianism suggests political force ensuring the rigidity of social norms, keeping everyone in his or her place, the problem with authoritarianism is the way that it manages the world and people as if it were managing a machine. In other words, humanity is denied. In the authoritarian regime, who a person is never exceeds what she is, and all attempts for this excess to make an appearance are ruthlessly crushed. On this understanding, the most familiar forms of authoritarianism may, indeed, be political systems where the vast majority of individuals have no say in how decisions are made. But there are many other means, probably more effective because more insidious than the formally political, by which the vast majority of individuals are disenfranchised, and by which social roles are made rigid. The real issue is how we see the world and how we see ourselves. We do so through forms of mediation, through concepts, words, images, and performances, as well as modern media technologies. Authoritarianism refers to a certain relationship we have with these forms of mediation, a certain confidence that they get the world right. Inevitably, these forms of mediation will reflect the interests of some and not of others, specifically, the interests of a wealthy and powerful minority. When forms of mediation are naturalized, they become a straightjacket worn by the 99 percent, crafted by the 1 percent, affirming the status of the 1 percent. Certainly political elites play a role in tightening and administering these straightjackets, but they are not decisive. Ideas circulate, through myth and media, through rumor and instruction, with good intentions and with bad.

If authoritarianism refers to holding in place the world and self on penalty of pain, democracy refers to the ability to challenge the views of world and self that we are given. The place to look for democracy is neither the realm of the spectator nor the realm of elites; it is in the middle, at the level of mediation. It is the mechanisms of mediation that hold world and self in place more or less tightly, that confirm the power of the few more or less strongly. Democracy begins to be actualized when individuals realize they are more than what they are told they are; it is fully actualized when the people, collectively, can change the way the world is represented. Instead of mediation constraining the people, the people in a democracy invent new forms of mediation—new concepts, words, images, performances, and technologies. A key mechanism through which this occurs is democratic charisma. It demonstrates that self and world are more than they seem, and it encourages others to realize the same. In other words, it primes the people for democratic transformation. The charismatic performance prepares its witnesses to challenge the ideas and images that have a hold on a society, the ideas and images that advance the interests of the few. It is not the individual with extraordinary charisma who leads the charge for transformation. It is the people themselves who can affect this transformation, who have always had the ability to affect this transformation. Each individual always has known and always will know that she is more than how the world describes her, that the ideas given to her by the world are deeply inadequate and unjust. Everyone knows this in private; the charismatic performer says it, or rather shows it, in public. When the secret is out in the open, ordinary people can act together, can fight together—this is what democracy looks like.

In some ways this account of democratic charisma turns classical accounts of charisma on their head. Social theorists following Max Weber often portray charisma as one model of authority, opposing it to traditional and legal-rational authority. Where traditional authority defers to the wisdom of past generations and to those who represent past generations in the present, legal-rational authority follows the rules written or affirmed in the present. The leaders of a society with traditional authority are often the descendants of past leaders, holding seemingly unlimited power to interpret community norms and values. In contrast, legal-rational authority places bureaucrats in charge of carrying out the norms codified through a formal process. These bureaucrats execute the laws in their professional capacities, whereas traditional leaders exercise their authority because of who they are, with little distinction between their public and private personas. The charismatic type of authority is wielded by a leader who demonstrates extraordinary, seemingly otherworldly abilities. Because of these abilities, she is respected, and her society allows her to determine its normative structure. Charismatic authority can be transformative, with the gifted leader quickly upending long-established social norms. However, charismatic authority also tends to be fleeting. After the charismatic leader dies, either her authority is transmitted to her descendants, shifting from charismatic to traditional authority, or her authority is codified and implemented by bureaucrats, shifting from charismatic to legal-rational authority. Either way, the social upheavals brought about by the presence of a charismatic leader come to an end along with the life of the leader.

This account of authority offered by social theorists is descriptive rather than normative, and one can easily see advantages and disadvantages to each of the three types. More interesting than adjudicating between them is reflecting on authority itself. We normally understand an authority as one to whom we cede our ability to judge because we trust the judgment of the authority more than we trust our own judgment. Democracy is inherently suspicious of authority: the only legitimate authority is the authority of the people, individually and collectively, and if that authority is delegated such delegation always remains provisional, with temporary authorities appointed by and reporting to the people. If this is how authority is understood in democracy, traditional authority would seem to be disqualified unless "the people" is understood in an unusually expansive way: Chesterton famously defines tradition as giving a vote to the dead. Legal-rational authority could clearly function in a democracy, with formal mechanisms for consulting the people and for holding their designees accountable. Weber and others flirted with the possibility of charismatic authority in a democracy, where a charismatic leader would be confirmed or removed from office in an occasional plebiscite but would hold relatively expansive powers, based on her apparently extraordinary gifts, while in office. But this is not what is meant here by democratic charisma.

The problem, again, has to do with mediation. Social theorists of authority ask to whom the people defer, particularly on issues of governance. If the people defer to no one, this is a democracy. But in fact the people continually and inevitably defer to the cultural substance that mediates our relationships and our lives: we defer to the set of words, images, performances, and technologies that are available to us. We have no choice, they must be employed if we are to engage with the world or with ourselves. This cultural substance is authoritative in the sense that it presents us with a set of options for how to see world and self, and no matter how frustrated we are with these limited options we must employ them. Such authority is much broader than, for example, the authority of the legal-rational bureaucrat who extracts taxes and dispenses parking tickets. It is not confined to certain spheres of life but affects them all. In this way it would seem closely related to traditional authority, with culture and tradition kissing cousins. Societies employing traditional modes of authority do give their leaders expansive powers to interpret what ought to be done in the present in light of the past, but diachronic tradition and synchronic cultural mediation differ in important ways. It is possible to argue about tradition, to tell a community's history in different ways that privilege different values, and tradition forms a shared, explicit point of reference in the community's normative discourse. In contrast, the authority of cultural mediation often is transparent, going undiscussed and uncontested. It is so essential that it is easy to overlook, particularly when alternative conceptual schemes or performative repertoires are unknown. Further, even if there were ongoing discussions about the way cultural mediation shapes a community's normative world, it is not clear how this authority would be contested. Certain images or words or technologies might be privileged to advance new normative positions, but there are tight constraints on the amount of flexibility this would provide.

The account of charismatic authority often provided in social theory has little room for the expansive power of mediation. Because of this, the charismatic mode of authority, as developed in social theory, usually refers to authoritarian charisma. A community cedes its capacity for reason and judgment on public affairs to a figure who seems to have extraordinary abilities. This is, indeed, how authoritarian charisma works, and it elides the cultural mediation that always accompanies charisma—and so it is necessarily undemocratic, indeed antidemocratic. The charismatic individual to whom authority is ceded often embodies, rather than transforms, the values of a community. In this case, charismatic authority and traditional authority are no different except that traditional authority allows for explicit debate about those values.

When the individual to whom authority is ceded does effect a significant transformation of her society, this does not imply making society anew ex nihilo, as the social theorist often implies. Such an account would be theological in the worst sense: it would posit that a new way of ordering a society drops down from the heavens into the mind of the charismatic leader. In reality, the charismatic leader who seems to introduce a radical reordering actually creatively misreads tradition. After all, the leader is constituted by tradition, having been reared in the community and versed in its history and values. Rather than assuming the role of the wise community elder, this sort of charismatic leader, who wields the most frightening type of authoritarian charisma, amplifies certain aspects of tradition and mutes others. The paradigms of evil charisma fall into this pattern: Jim Jones brings together racial unity, patriarchy, and paranoia; Idi Amin mobilizes traditional African religious practice together with cronyism and violence; or, most famous of all, Adolf Hitler weaves threads of nationalism, anti-Semitism, and Germanic mythology. In either the case of the charismatic leader who embodies tradition or the case of the charismatic leader who perverts tradition, charismatic authority must be explained in terms of cultural mediation—the only other explanation is the bogus popular psychological turn to the father-substitute. A community defers to the charismatic leader because they recognize their values, and the potential fulfillment of their desires, in the charismatic leader. To understand how this is the case, we need both to know something about the community's values and to know something about the forms in which those values can be articulated—whether by a particular style of public address or a certain television persona or missives from a mountaintop.

I have charged that the charismatic mode of authority depends on culture in a way that social theorists rarely allow. I further claim that the authority of democratic charisma is a particularly democratic mode of authority. Legal-rational and traditional modes of authority, as well as authoritarian charisma, depend on but ignore cultural mediation, yet cultural mediation is at the heart of democracy. If cultural mediation is ignored or reinforced (one product of ignoring it), it becomes all the more rigid, and a community moves away from democracy.

Democratic charisma is defined by the way in which it short-circuits cultural mediation, calling attention to the contingency and specificity of the concepts, words, images, performances, and technologies that define self and world. Does democratic charisma represent a mode of authority? It does, but in a way that forces us to understand authority differently. Democratic charisma does not name a type of charisma held by political elites. In fact, if there is charisma characteristic of elites, it would be decidedly undemocratic because it would be the charisma that accompanies playing a prescribed role (that of political elite) very well—in other words, it would be authoritarian charisma. Those who witness democratic charisma do, however, change because of the experience. They follow the charismatic figure in a very specific sense: they are motivated to share in her interrogation of the way the world and the self appear. The authority of democratic charisma is not deference to the beliefs or skills of another individual. It is deference to the process of critical inquiry, inquiry performed by the charismatic figure and joined in by those who witness her performance. As I have noted repeatedly, this critical inquiry can only be conducted, and performed, through cultural mediation, and it must at once use and question those forms of mediation. Figures of democratic charisma, whether they are singers or neighbors, podcasters or grandparents, call those who witness them out of dogmatic slumber. Their authority breaks old habits of seeing and talking and acting, making room for the new. Such figures of democratic charisma may seem far removed from the political domain, but they are essential to democracy. They are essential to a people who rules itself, essential to a person who would rule herself, for without such figures of democratic charisma a people is ruled by the ever more rigid networks of concepts and images, performances and technologies that dominate our lives.

To return to the theological idiom: authoritarian charisma implies idolatry, worship of human-constructed objects or ideas. Idolatry may seem democratic—the idol may be accepted by popular vote—but in fact idolatry, like authoritarian charisma, is antidemocratic. In ordinary usage the words *idol* and *charisma* are quite closely related. We often say that charismatic figures are idolized. The television show *American Idol* searches the nation for ordinary people with extraordinary gifts: people with musical charisma. When the Israelites grew frustrated with their charismatic leader, Moses, they built an idol, a golden calf, that they worshiped instead of the God who spoke through Moses. Idols have a quasi-divine character, where this sometimes has a negative connotation (the idol in competition with the divine) and sometimes is merely descriptive (the idol pointing to the extraordinary). The idol has powers beyond those usually found in the human world, but those powers are not gifts from God. They are secular, worldly, and they threaten to distract from God. Of course such distinctions overlook one that is rather more obvious. Idols are objects; charisma is an attribute of human beings. While the terms may be applied more broadly, such extended usage is metaphorical. However, when charisma is understood in what Rieff calls the "spray-on" sense, when it is authoritarian charisma at issue, charisma applies just as easily to an object—and charisma ultimately names a form of idolatry.

Idols attract undue attention. Those who view them look too closely and for too long. They return again and again to the idol, always finding their desires fulfilled, always leaving with even greater desire. The gold of a golden calf attracts the eye, offers it a shiny satisfaction that pleases, and cultivates the desire for more shininess. In short, idols distort our relationship with our world. They promise fulfillment themselves and so we overvalue them while undervaluing what we ought to care about. There is no need to believe in a God competing with the idol for our attention; it is enough to see how the idol captures our gaze and makes us neglect the world. Put another way, the easy satisfaction offered by the idol mutes our critical capacities. We do not need to reason or to map our experiences onto concepts when we stare at the idol. Its appearance alone, without thought or calculation on our part, brings us pleasure. This is precisely how authoritarian charisma works. It offers us something to look at, a performance that dazzles but that mutes our critical capacities. It gives us something we want while requiring little effort, and it leaves us wanting more. The more we are drawn in, the more we forget what mediates our experience of the idol, and the more we are focused exclusively on the object itself.

I say "object" here intentionally: we relate to the individual with authoritarian charisma as we relate to an object with similar properties because authoritarian charisma forecloses the human. The more charismatic, the less human: the human recedes as the charismatic individual becomes no more than an object attracting and organizing our desires: an idol. Recognizing the humanity of the one who has charisma, recognizing her idiosyncrasies and imperfections, would be a blemish distracting from the smooth, slick surface we expect from authoritarian charisma. In contrast, democratic charisma embraces the human. It leverages rather than conceals the dissonance between ordinary human being and extraordinary ability, reminding witnesses that humanity always thwarts our expectations.

Jean-Luc Marion has carefully reflected on the distinction between the idol and the icon, suggesting that the latter is an object or artwork that draws us toward the divine. Understanding the icon in this way does not require a belief in an otherworldly God. Rather, the icon draws us outside of ourselves. It

makes us reevaluate who we are and how we see the world—
quite different from the idol's implicit affirmation of who we
are and how we see the world. The icon represents the divine by
thwarting our attempts to represent, by attracting our gaze only
to solicit critical interrogation of that gaze, and ultimately humility. We think we can see the world rightly, that we can make
sense of all that we encounter, but we cannot. Democratic charisma takes the icon one step further. An icon is still an object,
not a human being, limiting the extent to which it can genuinely
surprise. The icon is instrumental, a tool that can challenge how
we see the world and our confidence in ourselves. Democratic
charisma is the icon embodied, perfected. Indeed, in that classic
story of charisma, the golden calf was opposed to Moses, the
imperfect human being whose communication was always mediated through Aaron, not opposed to an icon. Embodied, charisma is contagious. It not only has an effect on the viewer's
self-understanding, it offers a model for the viewer to replicate,
a way for the viewer herself to become charismatic and to spread
charisma to those who view her. Icons are enshrined in temples
and museums whereas charisma at its best, democratic charisma, lives in the courts and the slums, the halls of power and
prison corridors, in the young and old, the healthy and sick, the
immigrant and the exile—in the human.

Such democratic charisma involves inwardness but not authenticity. Authenticity implies some positive content, implies that
there is a proper way to be yourself. The inwardness of democratic charisma is entirely negative. It marks the inability to express one's self, the inability to ever find words or actions that
fully match who we are. In a way, inwardness and authenticity
are directly opposed to each other. The desire for authenticity
suggests a desire to conform outward actions to inner self. Inwardness is less a desire than a fact. It acknowledges that just as

words are part of a finite, contingent vocabulary that does not match the world and certainly does not match our selves, human actions are part of cultural repertoires that are equally contingent and finite. Inwardness calls attention to such finitude, rejecting all attempts to get the self right. To know thyself is an equivocal desire. It could mean a process without end or it could mean an achievable outcome. Authenticity is committed to the latter interpretation, inwardness to the former. In the how-to books purporting to teach charisma, those Rieff derisively labels as promoting "spray-on" charisma, authenticity is a key ingredient. Knowing who you are and being who you are is said to give you the confidence to achieve that magnetic personality you crave, to make you a leader of your peers. This is precisely charisma in its authoritarian form. Charisma that derives from authenticity is charisma that derives from a confidence about identity, an assurance that I have the capacity to make my words and my actions match who I am. In other words, authoritarian charisma achieves its power by advertising a way to make the world fit together perfectly, by advertising a self perfectly integrated with the world, representing itself flawlessly. Democratic charisma marks necessary flaws and asks that they be investigated; authoritarian charisma conceals flaws so as to make it seem that the world as it is matches the world as it ought to be, naturalizing hierarchies and inequities.

3

CHARISMA AND GOODNESS

Perhaps there is no man more closely identified with American goodness than Atticus Finch, the protagonist of Harper Lee's *To Kill a Mockingbird*. He cares about his family, about his community, and about what is right. It is impossible to imagine him doing anything wrong. If it seems as though he is doing wrong, it must be our perception that is mistaken. Atticus projects strength, consistency, and generosity; indeed, he seems to have all of the virtues in abundance. He is part of a community, but he is also above that community; specifically, he embodies the best in that community. Among Atticus's admirable qualities is his concern for those less fortunate. This concern manifests especially vividly with regard to that most vexing American moral challenge, the challenge of race. If only all white Americans were like Atticus Finch, it seems, racism would no longer be the nation's incurable disease. This is why so many American high school students read or watch *To Kill a Mockingbird*: to strengthen the moral fiber of the nation. Atticus, it would seem, understands freedom, equality, and justice better than anyone else; he becomes the father all white Americans wish they had. He becomes the father of the nation.

Atticus Finch is not only a paradigm of goodness, he is also a paradigm of charisma. Those around him, and those school children who encounter him today, are in awe. He is larger than life, extraordinary, possessing virtue to an extent unheard of in a mere mortal. Atticus occupies a position that calls for charisma, that of the lawyer, but it is clear that his charisma is more than the slickness usually associated with the lawyer. It is something about his presence, his being, that captivates not only a jury but also fellow townspeople, his children, and children today whose relationship with Atticus is mediated through text, screen, and the setting of the classroom. The charisma of a management guru, a politician, a singer, or even a preacher may be superficial, but surely the charisma of Atticus Finch is what charisma should be, charisma with depth and power, charisma that deserves to be treated as authoritative. Surely Atticus Finch has moral charisma.

But who is this revered man, Atticus Finch? A very specific image comes to mind—the image of another man, Gregory Peck. The Hollywood superstar's image is hard to separate from the image of Atticus Finch, the character he played exceptionally well, winning an Academy Award and a Golden Globe. Peck had played quintessentially American roles, replete with goodness and charisma: he was Captain Ahab in *Moby Dick*, an American journalist in love with a princess in *Roman Holiday*, a World War II pilot in *Twelve O'Clock High*, and a reporter posing as a Jew to reveal and overcome anti-Semitism in *Gentleman's Agreement*. The film *To Kill a Mockingbird*, released in 1962, puts Peck at its center. He is the strong, wise, and just father, lawyer, and fellow citizen. Peck's charisma matches and amplifies the charisma of Atticus Finch, and the medium—the Hollywood film—amplifies Peck's charisma and so doubly amplifies Atticus's, to the point that the essence of the film becomes the charisma of its protagonist, a charisma that offers the potential to save vulnerable children and to redeem a nation stained by racial injustice.

When Harper Lee's novel *Go Set a Watchman*—really an old novel, written as an early draft of *To Kill a Mockingbird*—surfaced and was quickly published in 2015, many readers were taken aback by the Atticus Finch they found. He was a lawyer and a father and a leading citizen of his small Southern town, but he was neither good nor charismatic. He disapproved of racial integration, spoke badly of blacks, and played a central role in his town's white citizens' council. Atticus had his reasons, largely pragmatic, and he claimed to disagree on many points with the racism of his peers, but this Atticus could by no means serve as the moral exemplar so many Americans had grown up with. He was, at the very least, complex and morally ambiguous. *Go Set a Watchman* offers no depiction of charisma. Atticus is a tired old man, worn down by the years, and he receives no particular attention or respect, and certainly not adoration, from those around him. Did Atticus's charisma and his goodness wear off in the two decades separating the setting of *To Kill a Mockingbird* and *Go Set a Watchman?*

If we turn to Harper Lee's classic novel itself, Atticus's charisma is rather more equivocal than it is often remembered, particularly when its memory is mediated by the overwhelming image of Gregory Peck. Lee is concerned with the tension between authoritarian charisma and democratic charisma; this is a central theme of *To Kill a Mockingbird* and even, in an importance sense, of *Go Set a Watchman*. The famous film transforms this fascinating exploration of equivocation into a performance of authoritarian charisma, identifying America with the powerful, white father figure who cares about justice but only when justice is accessible through the law of the land. In other words, that the film is dominated by authoritarian charisma means that it secures the (white supremacist, patriarchal) status quo, even if the most famous idea of the film is the necessity of empathy. This is the empathy of the helping hand, stretching down from the powerful to the marginalized, a helping hand that ultimately brings the marginalized into the (legal) system established by the powerful and so strengthens the chokehold that the powerful have on the marginalized.

There are certainly elements of authoritarian charisma associated with Atticus in Lee's *To Kill a Mockingbird*, elements that are amplified in the film version. Atticus is a father, strong and somewhat distant but also loving. The people of Maycomb recognize that he has a gift, that he is "not a run-of-the-mill man" (205). He operates in his own world, a world of the law, where he is respected, but he is happy to share his knowledge of the world with his two children, Scout and Jem. He teaches them to read and write even before they enter school. When Scout's teacher tells the girl that her father has taught her to read incorrectly, her father's authority trumps the authority of her teacher: Atticus declares that they can continue reading together. Atticus is a widower, making his authority in the household unquestioned; the black cook, Calpurnia, is clearly his subordinate, even as she orders the children around. Atticus is older than most of the fathers in the Maycomb community, and at first, from the children's perspective, it seems as though he has limited abilities. He does not seem to have the physical strength or manual skill of other men. Just as these thoughts cross the mind of his daughter, an incident changes Scout's perception. A rabid dog is wandering about town and Atticus is called. He shoots the dog, revealing a long-concealed skill: Atticus used to be the town's champion marksman. To the children, it is clear that Atticus is now a real, potent man: he can shoot a gun better than anyone else they know. This physical, phallic power is closely linked in the text with Atticus's legal power. From the children's naive perspective, it had seemed as though the law was impotent. There are no concrete objects or products involved in the legal profession. But the man who knows the law best can shoot the gun best, and the law itself has the power to save or destroy lives, and families.

In court, in the novel's climactic trial, Lee describes a sharp contrast between Atticus and his opposing counsel, the man prosecuting Tom Robinson. "There was a brown book and some yellow tablets on the solicitor's table; Atticus's was bare" (168). The prosecutor knows the law from books whereas Atticus embodies the law. Atticus has charisma without mediation: he needs no notes, no scholarship, no references; he just speaks the law. He just is the law. In his closing statement, bringing the trial of the black accused rapist Tom Robinson to an end, Atticus concludes with the words, "In the name of God, do your duty" (210). The next words, Atticus's last to the jury, he speaks very softly, and they are only made available for the reader (significantly) by his son's repetition of them: "In the name of God, believe him." Not only does Atticus stand in for the law at its most majestic, he stands as God's representative on earth, bringing a message to the people of Maycomb. The message, importantly, is not that Maycomb is a fallen land replete with sin, and it is not that there is a higher law that the jury ought to follow. Atticus rather sanctifies the laws of Maycomb, the laws already on the books. God, it seems, is not so interested in the content of law as in the existence of law, the moral duty to follow the law whatever it may be. The law must be followed in good faith: the testimony of each witness should be critically evaluated, evaluated without prejudice—this is what taking seriously the duty to follow the law means. It is a duty to God, a duty represented by Atticus, and a duty transmitted from generation to generation: a duty understood and repeated (for the reader) by Atticus's son.

Atticus not only represents the law, he also represents tradition, particularly tradition as it is purified and projected onto family history. Tradition in a broad sense may entail stories of the past with myriad social practices along with the values implicit in those practices, but tradition is often understood in a narrower sense. Tradition in this latter sense suggests that which is passed down from generation to generation—even more narrowly, from father to son, father to son. In the novel, the long history of the Finches in Maycomb, including the historic location, Finch's Landing, points to the way in which intergenerational transmission is entwined with community history. Atticus, in his role of father to a son, embodies this tradition and has the essential task of seeing that it continues vigorously into the future. What Atticus preserves, and what is always preserved with tradition, is not only history and values but also social hierarchy. As tradition is transmitted, so are roles transmitted—those who are cast in positions of power and those who are marginal are secured in those relative social positions because of tradition. One way of reading *To Kill a Mockingbird* is as a story of those at the margins becoming frustrated with their perpetual condemnation to these margins. The villain, Bob Ewell, has eight children, but he lacks the resources to support them, to raise them rightly. He lives just beyond the city dump, on the way to the black neighborhood. When Ewell is humiliated by Atticus in court, by means of a law he does not understand, he decides to have his revenge by attacking Atticus's children. In other words, Ewell attempts to cut off the intergenerational transmission that is at the heart of Maycomb tradition. If Atticus embodies tradition, and so his children embody the continuity of tradition, destroying those children is the best way to challenge the status quo, to disrupt the distribution of power in the community that leaves Ewell damned, next to the dump.

The Gregory Peck film accentuates the omnipotence and omniscience of Atticus. "There just didn't seem to be anything or anyone Atticus couldn't explain," we are told. He knew the ways of the world, the laws of the world, perfectly. Peck plays the role with an accent that fluctuates between generically American, Southern, and mid-Atlantic, emphasizing the sense that Atticus is Maycomb but also greater than it, more universal than it. He speaks clearly and precisely, with an air of formality equally present in the courtroom and on his front porch. His posture is perfect, his hair is perfect, and his clothes are perfect. When he speaks, those around him listen. He may not be young and vigorous, but in his middle age he is confident and wise. In court, his dark tie stands out boldly, phallically, against his white three-piece suit.

Atticus Finch is a man without secrets. What you see is what you get. There are no hints at inwardness. This is magnified by his filmic portrayal: on the big screen, played by a Hollywood star, what we see are surfaces. What makes the portrayal of Atticus so compelling is Gregory Peck's ability to make us believe that these surfaces go all the way down. He makes the audience believe that the physical appearance of integrity and speech that sounds like it has integrity really mark a man whose life is entirely characterized by integrity. He looks good, he speaks the truth, and he is good. In the novel, a neighbor reports, "Atticus Finch is the same in his house as he is on the public streets" (52). This is a sentiment that Atticus explicitly shares: "I can't live one way in town and another way in my home" (278). Charisma, classically, names an extraordinary gift, seemingly from the heavens. It is a gift that is ultimately illegible to the world; that illegibility intrigues. Atticus is extraordinary, but his gift is entirely legible. There is no mystery whatsoever: it is goodness on top, goodness in the middle, and goodness down below. We cannot imagine being surprised by Atticus. (It is also hard to imagine him telling a joke.) This is authoritarian charisma: what seems like a divine gift is actually just the values of a culture projected onto one particular individual.

While *To Kill a Mockingbird* is often thought to be centrally concerned with justice, or with a law that is higher than the law of the land, in fact the novel and film take the meaning of justice to be following the law properly. The law is something abstract but also solid and comforting—just like Atticus himself. While the children in the story may be mischievous, their adventures never contest the rules of the father. When those rules are broken, infractions are acknowledged. Atticus himself is meticulous about following gentlemanly norms, for example, when he consistently greets with kindness an ornery neighbor. When his children do not follow his model of courtesy, he sentences them to assist the elderly neighbor, enduring her hostility. It seems to the children that the woman's treatment of them is unjust, but Atticus prioritizes the customary courtesy of the South. After the trial that forms the centerpiece of the story, Atticus and Jem discuss how the legal system needs to change to be more just. They consider whether it would be better to have judges, rather than juries, render verdicts in capital cases, or whether perhaps juries should render a verdict and then judges should set the punishment. In other words, the discussion revolves around how to make the law work better, more smoothly. They do not acknowledge the possibility of a fundamental mismatch between worldly law and higher ideals of justice. Commitment to worldly law, even if that law may need to be revised, is a central

feature of authoritarian charisma. Such charisma does not disrupt the ways of the world, it secures them. Charismatic authority in this sense is not an alternative to legal-rational or
traditional authority; it reinforces both those types of authority.
Indeed, *To Kill a Mockingbird* illustrates how charismatic authority can join together legal-rational and traditional authority. As
both novel and film remind us, Atticus is from a respectable family, and preserving that respectability, that tradition of good
blood, as it were, is imperative. Atticus is also committed to a
system of law and order that functions properly, impartially. One
way of reading the central conflict of the book is to highlight how
the tension between traditional authority and legal-rational
authority faced by Atticus when doing his job, lawyering, will
bring disrepute on his family. The family name would be diminished if it is associated with defending blacks, but the authority of law will be diminished if Atticus refuses to defend
Tom Robinson—a tragic choice.

It takes the charisma of Atticus Finch to supersede this conflict. Because of his charisma, and the way it makes Maycomb
view him, Atticus is able to resist the threat to the dignity of his
family name posed by his commitment to the law. Instead of
deferring to either legal-rational authority or traditional authority, Atticus affirms both by affirming himself, specifically, his
conscience. As he describes it, conscience is the highest authority of all. But conscience here does not refer to some aspect
of our humanity that cannot be captured by the outside world,
that cannot be represented. Rather, conscience simply marks
what unifies legal-rational authority and traditional authority,
and it is the display of conscience that produces the effect of
charisma. In other words, authoritarian charisma here is the simulacrum of democratic charisma. It is as if charisma is produced
by accessing the human, by thwarting attempts at representing

the human, but actually charisma is produced by perfectly representing a society's view of humanity. Authoritarian charisma is produced by unifying the law's definition of humanity and tradition's definition of humanity in one person, one conscience. If charisma is to strengthen the status quo, this requires reconciling the conflicting forces that give shape to the status quo: reason and laws systematically applied, on the one hand, and a community's values implicit in its history and cultural practices, on the other. This is the task so successfully accomplished by Atticus Finch.

So far, Harper Lee's protagonist does seem to display the authoritarian charisma familiar from the film. But Lee's portrayal of Atticus is more complicated. She repeatedly emphasizes how he is old and sedentary, how he spends his spare time reading and doing little else. He does shoot a gun well, once, but for the most part Atticus is not a leading specimen of Maycomb manliness. Indeed, his wife has been dead for a few years and he seems to have no interest in remarriage; eventually, his prim sister comes to manage the household. (In contrast, in the film version Atticus is on quite friendly terms with an attractive, widowed neighbor, played by Rosemary Murphy; his sister is not depicted.) Atticus's extended family thinks that he is not capable of raising his children on his own; he needs assistance. Further, there is something rather mysterious about Atticus, and there are portions of his life to which the reader is never made privy. For example, we are told that he is a state legislator, and that this takes him away from Maycomb for extended periods of time, but we learn nothing of his political life. Even though Atticus is committed to the law, he is a lawyer rather than a judge. He is willing to interpret the law creatively to advance the interests of his clients—for example, reaching the "compromise" of reading with Scout at home even after Scout's teacher has prohibited it.

Atticus makes quite explicit his views of human nature. All people, even the lowly and even the seemingly vicious, are essentially good, but all people have "blind spots" (161). The theme of empathy, often touted as the core lesson taught by the novel, is really a lesson about overcoming those blind spots in ourselves. Our judgment is always distorted. To restore it, Atticus famously recommends walking in another's shoes. But he says more than this: he commends accessing the human in the other. From the outside, we can see what a person is, but it is only from the inside, as it were, that we can see who they are. This answer to the question of "who" cannot return to the level of discourse and representation. It is the answer to the question of the human, an answer that is at once ineffable and transcendent. Atticus approaches this answer from another direction when he responds to his daughter's statement, concerning the Tom Robinson case, that "most folks seem to think they're right and you're wrong"—"They're certainly entitled to think that . . . but before I can live with other folks I've got to live with myself. The one thing that doesn't abide by majority rule is a person's conscience" (110–111). To know what is right, one has to look inside oneself, to look at who one is. To know how to treat another, then, one has to find out both who one is and who the other is, refusing the shorthands offered by language and culture that only answer the question of what one is. Indeed those shorthands can lead astray: they create ethics by election, by majority vote, posing questions in the abstract without considering the significance of the human, of human dignity.

Atticus makes these remarks in conversation with his children, one type of charismatic performance; they can also be taken to animate the charismatic scenario of the trial. Lee portrays Atticus in the courtroom quite differently than the role is performed by Gregory Peck. As Lee tells it, Atticus is not a

particularly animated speaker, nor does he tell the most atten-
tion-grabbing stories. He is careful and steady, but the result is that
he solicits from his audience, particularly the jury but also the
courtroom as a whole (including, significantly, his children), an
awareness of the humanity of another—and so an opportunity
to recognize anew audience members' own humanity. Atticus
does not give the jury what they expect from a charismatic trial
lawyer: a powerful voice, riveting arguments, and pregnant
pauses. He does not appeal to their preexisting desires to be,
effectively, entertained by charisma. "Things were utterly dull:
nobody had thundered, there were no arguments between
opposing counsel, there was no drama. . . . Atticus was proceed-
ing amiably, as if he were involved in a title dispute" (173). Atticus's charisma works, in the novel, by frustrating the jury's, and
the audience's, and the reader's desires and so making them reevaluate their desires. It would seem as if a case of black-on-
white rape in the early-twentieth-century American South
would evoke tremendous passions. By treating it passionlessly,
Atticus startles his audience and causes them to question why
such passions are normally evoked. He invites them to treat this
case as they would treat the most mundane, a title dispute,
which means looking at Tom Robinson as they would look at
anyone else—as they would look at a white man. Lee's narrator
describes Atticus's oration, significantly, as "dry as a sermon"
(173). Just because a speech is dry does not mean it is insignifi-
cant; a sermon, after all, has grave significance to its audience.
In the same way that Atticus asks his audience to consider their
God-given duty, to treat Tom Robinson as human, his ser-
monic mode of presentation emphasizes that this duty is God-
given. Once again, this thwarts the expectations and desires of
the audience. They want salacious detail and breathless exhor-
tations; what they receive is more serious, more religious, and it

reminds them that they are capable of more than being entertained by tabloid fodder.

During his closing argument, Atticus does something his children have never seen him do before, something they imagined he had never done before in public. After asking permission from the judge, he takes his coat off. The jury was used to seeing Atticus in a particular way, as a leading Maycomb attorney, dressed for the part. The people of Maycomb, including even Atticus's children, had not seen him simply as a man, as a human being. By taking his jacket off, this is the identification he invites. His ultimate goal is not for the jury to see his humanity, but to remind the jury that everyone, behind their outer garments, beyond their skin color, beneath the ways they are usually represented, has something more. Each has something exceeding representation, exceeding descriptions—that is the human. And it is contagious. Once it is spotted in one place, it is spotted in others. Once the jury begins to consider the human in Atticus, they are primed to see the human not only in themselves but, crucially, in Tom Robinson. We are told in the novel that Atticus "walked slowly up and down in front of the jury, and the jury seemed to be attentive: their heads were up, and they followed Atticus's route with what seemed to be appreciation" (206). Even though Atticus was not shouting, he had prompted the jury to see him anew and, through the effects of democratic charisma, to see Tom Robinson anew, or at least this was the hope.

Lee portrays Atticus's charisma as ambivalent, in some ways authoritarian and in other ways democratic. But Atticus is not the only charismatic character in the novel. Indeed, there is a sense in which the novel, unlike the film, does not portray Atticus as uniquely charismatic at all. At the end of the day, he loses the climactic court case (even if the jury deliberates for longer than expected), and he is not even able to protect his own family from the revenge sought by Bob Ewell. Atticus's children survive Ewell's violence, but this is thanks to the help of their reclusive neighbor, Boo Radley. In contrast, Scout, whose person and voice are at the center of the novel, does cause a real effect in the world. Unlike her father, she succeeds in saving Tom Robinson's life and persuading a group of Maycomb citizens to change their ways. Specifically, when a mob of angry Maycomb citizens comes in the middle of the night to lynch Tom Robinson, Atticus's attempts to hold off the crowd come to naught. They are determined to capture and kill the black man accused of raping a white woman. As the crowd is about to break into the jail, Scout and her young friends enter the scene. Scout does not directly try to persuade the mob to go home. She knows something is amiss, and she intuits injustice. She begins talking to one particular member of the mob. She tells Walter Cunningham that she goes to school with his son and that she remembers her father worked on a case for him, and she inquires about his family. He is left speechless, the mob's frenzy calms, and Tom Robinson survives. Scout's speech persuades because it reminds the lynch mob that they are more than how they represent themselves. They have other lives, with jobs, and families, and problems of their own. Scout's words do not persuade by feeding some desire of Cunningham and his fellows, a desire that would be even stronger than their desire for a lynching. She persuades by inviting the lynch mob to probe their own desires, to probe their own humanity beyond the way that they see themselves. This is democratic charisma.

It might seem as though Scout's innocence is essential to her persuasiveness. The angry mob is reminded to think of the children: Scout, Jem, their friend Dill, Cunningham's boy, and all the other young people of Maycomb. In other words, it might seem as though children are naturally gifted with democratic charisma because they prompt those who hear their words to remember a time when their own humanity was purer, uncorrupted by the violent and prejudiced ways of the world, when each could see one another unencumbered. But this cannot quite be the case. It would suggest that children have charisma that succeeds because it is unmediated, because it can directly express humanity without soiling itself with the complications of culture. But mediation is essential to democratic charisma: it is by engaging with mediation that the limits of mediation are revealed, and that the human is revealed. Authoritarian charisma feeds on a fantasy of the unmediated, of the god who speaks into our ear. Scout does not speak pure truth to the lynch mob. She performs cultural conventions: she uses the familiar greeting "Hey, Mr. Cunningham," asks Cunningham to convey her greetings to his son ("Tell him hey for me, won't you"), and so on (156–157). She employs familiar Maycomb social practices in a way that calls attention to the contingency of social practices and the humanity they conceal. (Lynching, after all, is also a Maycomb social practice.)

It is not quite right to regard children as having democratic charisma because they have not yet mastered the norms of a community. If democratic charisma depends on calling into question such norms, using forms of mediation against themselves to display the human, fluency in a language and a full array of cultural practices is a prerequisite for democratic charisma. The child-king or child-saint may be treated as holy, but this is clearly an example of authoritarian charisma. In such cases, the child, largely mute, is adored because of the social hierarchies that she represents and reinforces. (Facebook pictures of babies have much the same effect, purified by the additional layer of technological mediation.) Scout certainly does not have this sort of authoritarian charisma, but at her young age, with her naïveté about the world, her democratic charisma would seem to be, at most, quite limited. Much of the time, the town does not take notice of her, and she is treated as just one of the many Maycomb children. It is only in the tense moment in front of the town jail when Scout's limited familiarity with Maycomb cultural practices succeeds, perhaps by chance, in achieving democratic charisma.

Yet Scout is more than just one of the Maycomb children in *To Kill a Mockingbird*, and the audience for her charisma is not just the Maycomb adults. She is also the book's narrator, speaking to readers. Indeed, she wears two hats simultaneously, that of mature narrator recalling her childhood in the past tense and that of naive but feisty child navigating her way about town and learning the intricacies of Maycomb culture. It is out of this dual role that Scout's charismatic power, her democratic charisma, emerges. She is at once wise to the world and innocent. That these two voices can exist in the same person, simultaneously, restrains the audience (the reader) from becoming too comfortable with either. Its effect is to remind the reader of the contingency of cultural practices and the way that our humanity exceeds any reduction to our cultural context. It marks inwardness. We are reminded that the narrator, the adult Scout, was formed by the constantly unfolding (and so effectively limitless) layers of her youthful experience, that no attempt to describe the adult Scout will ever get her right because of the richness and import of those unknown experiences. Similarly, in the voice of the youthful Scout, we are reminded that there was an individual who existed before she was fully acculturated into the ways of Maycomb, and the world, and that this process of acculturation took time and violence and tears. In short, with Scout's two voices in one, we are reminded of the contingency of culture and the way humanity exceeds representation; we, as readers, find the book compelling because we recognize this in ourselves. We are prompted to recognize the human in us. This is precisely the pedagogical message announced in the novel's epigraph: "Lawyers, I suppose, were children once." We adults who know the law, who effortlessly navigate cultural practices, are at the same time more than we seem. There is no way to return and no way to give a complete account of this excess. But speaking at once as a child and as an adult reminds us that we are more than we seem, even to ourselves.

The Scout character (and so the narrative voice of the novel) is split in other ways as well. She has an ambivalent gender identity marked by her names: "Jean Louise" and "Scout" are used interchangeably by those around her. She likes playing with the boys, and her aunt is concerned that she is not learning properly how to be a woman. Scout resists her aunt's pressure to feminize, but not entirely, and she does enter more deeply into the life of the Maycomb ladies. *Go Set a Watchman* further explores this process and features a storyline that underscores this gender ambivalence. The young Scout has a male friend who takes her to the school dance. She buys a dress but feels uncomfortable about her boyish figure, so she purchases artificial breasts. Unfortunately, they move out of place during the dance, humiliating her. Her young suitor, Jack, says that the breasts are unnecessary and throws them away, into the schoolyard. They are found the next day, angering the school principal, who demands a confession. (The demand is undermined when all of the girls write confessions.) The evening of the dance ends with Scout pleased to receive a kiss from her suitor; in the present-tense narrative of *Go Set a Watchman*, Scout is still undecided about whether she wants to be romantically involved with this same suitor (who is, significantly, Atticus's apprentice, representing a continuity in the family line). While some critics have read Scout as an example of the literary "queer child," Scout's gender ambivalence could also be read as echoing her two voices, and similarly pointing to a humanity beneath. As Scout, she is positioned within the male lineage of the Finches, and of Maycomb; as Jean Louise, she is subject to the equally strict cultural codes governing ladylike behavior. By acknowledging but also refusing to fully embrace both sets of norms without wallowing in ambivalence, Scout/Jean Louise again invites the reader, and on occasion the people of Maycomb, to reflect on what it means to be human beyond gendered and other cultural codes.

Lee portrays this character, her real protagonist, as having little affective investment in gender identity or sexuality. In Scout's early twenties, her relationship with Jack is still unsettled, but this does not particularly worry her. She may marry him or she may not. Similarly, she was not eager to participate in ladies' social gatherings in Maycomb—not because they were for ladies, but because they were tedious. Scout has a similarly unaffected response to learning the facts of life later than her peers. As portrayed in *Go Set a Watchman*, Scout is concerned with the practicalities, worried that she might have become pregnant and would be sent away or would need to care for the child. In short, it is not as if Scout is suffering from affective tumult because of a "queer" identity. Her gender ambivalence is but one of the ambivalences that mark her as human.

Scout has yet another set of opposing identities. In *Go Set a Watchman*, she has moved to the North, away from the South, in which she was reared. The contemporary narrative in the novel follows Scout's return to Maycomb from the North, with the locals wondering about the Northern beliefs and customs she may have acquired. There is an obvious way in which Scout is functioning as a bridge between Northern readers and the

South that intrigues them, the South of their fantasies. Her name, after all, is just two letters away from South. But reading Scout in that way would suggest that she has authoritarian charisma, confirming preexisting beliefs and desires of Lee's Northern readers for Southern exoticism. In the novel, Scout describes the rough ways of New York City public transportation and continues, "They have manners, Claudine. They're just different from ours. The person who pushed me on the bus expected to be pushed back. That's what I was supposed to do; it's just a game" (181). Cultural practices are contingent; they should not be vested with heavy moral weight. Southerners and Northern readers should not judge one another too harshly and should not take themselves too seriously—after all, "it's just a game." Scout does not simply condense and rehearse a fantasized South for its other. She explores her self because she appreciates the contingencies of both Southern and Northern customs, and she invites readers into similar self-exploration.

This is too charitable a characterization of Lee's *Go Set a Watchman*. It is, after all, a novel that fails. It was rightly discarded in order to make way for a masterpiece. Why does the earlier novel fall short? *To Kill a Mockingbird* is concerned with democratic charisma, and it performs democratic charisma (it mediates Lee's charisma). *Go Set a Watchman* is concerned with deconstructing authoritarian charisma. This is a rather more laborious and technical project, and Lee often tends toward the pedantic, particularly at what the reader hopes would be the novel's climax. Where *To Kill a Mockingbird* usually reproduces short exchanges and describes longer speeches (those in court), *Go Set a Watchman* reproduces long speeches aimed at decisively demonstrating the shortcomings of authoritarian charisma. A quite plausible story could be told about how Lee needed first to deconstruct authoritarian charisma before she was able to represent, and express, democratic charisma. The spell of authoritarian charisma—the spell of the father—must be broken in order for the human to become visible.

The central plotline of *Go Set a Watchman* involves Scout learning that her father and his protégé (her sometime fiancé) are involved in a racist organization that Scout considers abominable, the Maycomb white citizens' council. She is enraged, her father tries to justify his actions, and finally her medical doctor uncle brings reconciliation, offering a psychological explanation for Scout's rage, which she accepts. Lee fully embraces the clichés of popular psychology when she describes Scout's relationship with her father. He was "the most potent moral force in her life. . . . She never questioned it, never thought about it, never even realized that before she made any decision of importance the reflex, 'What would Atticus do?' passed through her unconscious" (117). Atticus was the ultimate authority, and his authority was fully internalized by his daughter. When she learns that Atticus is involved in the racist council, she is crushed: "The one human being she had ever fully and wholeheartedly trusted had failed her" (113). Her normative world collapses; she is disoriented. Scout can engage with the rest of her world critically, often cynically, but when it comes to her father, she has either pure reverence or pure fury. When Scout's sometime fiancé describes a neighbor's love as blinding, Scout is quickly dismissive. "The sun rises and sets with that Bill of hers. Everything he says is Gospel. She loves her man." "Is that what loving your man is?" "Has a lot to do with it." "You mean losing your own identity, don't you?" (227).

That Scout is capable of realizing this is love gone wrong foreshadows her realization, aided by her uncle, that her own love for her father is problematic. At the same time, Lee also has Scout learn the lesson that, in the real world, it is often necessary for appearances and realities to mismatch. Her uncle explains to her that, in order to accomplish a noble objective, one must often align oneself with others who have less noble objectives. Some who participate in the citizens' council may be crude racists, aligned with the Ku Klux Klan, but many are also interested primarily in strengthening their community. Scout had imagined that being good means doing good all the time, speaking the truth, appearing beautiful, like her father, but she now apprehends that being good is more complicated. The world is more complicated. To fully engage with the world means navigating between shades of grey, Scout is learning. "A man can be boiling inside, but he knows a mild answer works better than showing his rage" (230). This, again, is a challenge to authoritarian charisma, to the desire for smoothness of presentation and of self-presentation, in the form of a challenge to Scout's perception of her father.

The transformation at the center of *Go Set a Watchman* is not only about the idealized image of a father breaking down. It is also about an idealized image of justice breaking down. Scout had seen her father as not only omniscient and omnipotent but also supremely just. As a lawyer, he was committed to using the law to advance justice, or so it seemed. In Scout's long diatribe against her father as her idealization collapses, she revisits the defense of Tom Robinson (alluded to but not described in detail in *Go Set a Watchman*). "You love justice, all right," Scout angrily tells her father. "Abstract justice written down item by item on a brief—nothing to do with that black boy, you just like a neat brief. His cause interfered with your orderly mind, and you had to work order out of disorder. It's a compulsion with you" (248). Scout is discovering that she confused law and justice. She thought that following the law properly, or if necessary improving the law, would always lead to justice. She had identified her father with justice, but actually her father was solely identified with law—for him, justice was reduced to a criminal justice system, a set of laws and procedures. Her father wanted an orderly world, wanted to be able to see everything and everyone fit together systematically, and law allowed him to do this. Law organizes the world, and it does so with normative force: it offers penalties for those who break it. Scout was intuitively concerned with justice, and through her life she satisfied this concern by deferring to her father, by deferring to the law. Now, a divide appears for her between justice and law, and it frustrates her. It seemed as though there was no higher authority than her father, unifying legal-rational and traditional authority with his charismatic authority. Now, she knows there must be a higher authority, but she is not sure where to turn. She contemplates eternal exile—as a Southerner, she is not at home in New York City, and her refuge in Maycomb that she thought of as her home, her father's house, no longer offers her a normative blanket for comfort.

Scout's uncle puts her predicament in explicitly religious terms: "You confused your father for God. You never saw him as a man with a man's heart, and a man's failings" (265). When we see another rightly, we evaluate his virtues and vices, his strengths and weaknesses. We appreciate that the way the world would have us see the other never captures who he is, never captures his "heart," his humanity. Authoritarian charisma depends on, and encourages, misrepresenting the world and dehumanizing others. The charismatic figure is seen as possessing an extraordinary gift from God, a gift so spectacular that humanity is concealed. It is because of that gift that we are to defer to her, to treat her, God's vessel, as a supreme authority. Such is the misrecognition of the father. Democratic charisma is what allows us to see that human heart, and it is democratic charisma to which Lee's next book is devoted. Hints at what such charisma would look like are provided in *Go Set a Watchman* by Scout's uncle, the man who urges her to look for the heart, for the human. This uncle was a medical doctor, but he retired early and now devotes himself to personal studies of Victorian literature and society. He is seen as somewhat of an eccentric, often digressing, often quoting obscure texts, an outlier in the community. But Dr. Finch is respected, by the town and by Scout. He helps Scout see her father rightly, and so opens her to seeing herself and her world differently, beyond the shadow of the father.

Dr. Finch brings *Go Set a Watchman* to a close by urging Scout to set aside her anger at her father, and he assures Scout that her father will hold no hard feelings (he does not). Instead of the life of an exile, Dr. Finch urges Scout to return permanently to Maycomb and to make the town a better place. She is perplexed: If the majority of the town's white residents are so misguided, how could she possible advance justice? Her uncle assures her, "I don't mean by fighting; I mean by going to work every morning, coming home at night, seeing your friends" (272). Justice, Dr. Finch is saying, does not come down from the mountaintop accompanied by thunder and lightning. It does not come from the father, and it does not come from the legal system. Justice comes about through being a good person, leading an ordinary life, treating others rightly. At the end of the day, this is how Atticus lives, too. Scout may perceive him as charismatic, but *Go Set a Watchman* does not suggest that anyone else in town does. He does his duty, tries to be good, and tries to treat others rightly, knowing that sometimes he will miscalculate, sometimes his hands will be uncomfortably soiled by the messiness of the town, of the world. The book closes with this invitation to democratic charisma that is made possible by the demystification of authoritarian charisma, but this is also what has been performed throughout the book. Besides Scout's relationship with her father, the novel is largely without charisma. In a sense, Lee does not yet know how to respond to the invitation to democratic charisma. She does not yet know what happens after the death of the father. The only response she can muster is an affirmation of the status quo. Indeed, Lee's own life after her moment in the spotlight suggests a return to such paralysis. While she was never a recluse, and she would occasionally make public appearances, she refused mediation: she would not be interviewed in the press, and she preferred to live her life in relative anonymity, in her hometown. As a white octogenarian in twenty-first century Alabama, she still had a black woman cooking her meals and taking care of her home, eerily reminiscent of the Calpernia character she created, Atticus's maid. Lee's instinct may have been to reject authoritarian charisma, and her later, quiet life with her sister but no husband was one way to do this, but her refusal to engage with mediation was a refusal of the democratic charisma suggested by *To Kill a Mockingbird* at its best. Her life followed Dr. Finch's advice to Scout, and it had the expected result: the attempt at advancing justice through the ordinary, by the privileged, perpetuated systemic injustice.

There is another way of approaching *To Kill a Mockingbird* that may offer another way to understand charisma's democratic potential. On this approach, if the film version is about charisma, the book is about charisma's opposite, disgrace. Charisma, classically, marks a divine gift, a gift of grace. Disgrace marks grace taken away, a human emptied of the divine. The distinction here is subtle. The lack of charisma in one sense simply suggests an individual fully determined by her culture. In such an individual, all of the human has been muted: she just does what is done, all the time. Yet this is impossible; or, rather, it is possible only in the abstract, in the realm of ideology where norms entirely match social practice. This cannot be disgrace. In reality, every actual human being is deeply complex, with a manifold history shaping her conscious and unconscious, with varied and conflicting desires, and with ambivalence toward aspects of the culture, community, and family in which she lives. What, then, is disgrace? It is the result of an attempt to express the human that goes wrong. Rather than displaying the human beyond expectations, and calling forth the human in others, disgrace results from an infelicitous attempt to push against cultural norms, an assertion of human will that only solicits condemnation. The disgraced public figure did more than follow the norms for her role, and this excess was fueled by self-interest or lack of self-discipline. She is condemned as bad, as untruthful, as morally if not physically ugly.

One who is disgraced repels rather than attracts. Those around her avoid her; conversations are quickly brought to an end when she enters. Unlike one who is shamed, there is no spectacle involved in disgrace. (Perhaps we could say that shame is to authoritarian charisma as disgrace is to democratic charisma.) Disgrace entails social isolation without even attracting the attention of those who would condemn. Where one who has charisma looks her interlocutors in their eyes, seeing their hearts, the eyes of one who is disgraced turn downward. She tried to show her humanity to the world, but she failed. Now, she wants no one to see who she is. Such disgrace is at the very heart of *To Kill a Mockingbird* and animates the novel's narrative, though it is largely absent from the film. Lee describes Maycomb as a community tightly organized around social expectations. People with the last name Cunningham are supposed to act a certain way; people with the last name Finch are supposed to act a different way; and so social order and hierarchy are enforced. There is a constant worry in the novel that Scout will be a disgrace, that she will not act as a proper Finch, that she will assert herself against her culture. (In *Go Set a Watchman* this worry is so internalized that Scout's pregnancy scare prompts her near-suicide.) The trial of Tom Robinson is essentially about disgrace. The community feels that Bob Ewell's daughter would have been disgraced by sexual intercourse with a black man, and this disgrace would have been doubled if the intercourse was consensual—the young woman's desire revealed an aspect of her humanity that went against cultural norms. She would not have lived up to her role as a proper white woman, a role that guarantees the little social standing that she has, given her family's poverty. At the trial, Ewell himself feels disgraced. It becomes clear that he orchestrated a lie under oath, spoken to the whole community assembled in the courtroom. Even more, it becomes clear that Ewell asserts himself by beating his adult daughter, considered by the community unbecoming of a fellow citizen.

The most significant instance of disgrace in the novel is a storyline about redemption, about the way disgrace and charisma are entwined, and are sometimes interchangeable. In his youth, Boo Radley committed a transgression, pushing beyond the limits of youthful iniquity by targeting a symbol of law, a policeman. While his co-conspirators were sent away, Radley's father would not have his family name associated with an institute for delinquents. Radley instead keeps Boo at home, but Boo never leaves the house. Atticus suggests that this is not because of physical restraints. It was not chains holding Boo to his bed; "there were other ways of making people into ghosts." Radley's father embodied the law, direct from God: "he was so upright he took the word of God as his only law. . . . Mr. Radley's posture was ramrod straight" (17). In the presence of the law, Boo Radley could only hide. Gossip in the town has it that he challenged this law once, suddenly stabbing his paternal guardian with scissors. With such an overbearing figure of law so close, all that the younger Radley could do to express himself was physically strike out.

Boo Radley forms an unlikely bond with Scout and the children of her circle, and he ultimately saves them from the violence of another disgraced townsman, Bob Ewell. On the standard reading, the novel teaches empathy for all forms of otherness, from the poor to the black to the mentally unstable, like Boo. But as a novel that is performing democratic charisma, featuring a protagonist, Scout, gifted with such charisma, the message of the novel has more to do with forging an alliance of singularities, of individual human beings who recognize that their humanity goes beyond how they are described by the world. This is how Scout's double voices are best understood, as pointing to her singularity, and it is through charismatic contagion that she can relate to another who is more than how the world perceives him. It takes time and critical engagement for Scout to see Boo Radley as more than the world sees him, but she eventually does—modeling the response that Lee solicits from her readers. Importantly, at the very end of the book, the only person who has trouble understanding that it was Boo Radley who saved the children's lives is Atticus, that embodiment of the law, and of tradition. The father thinks it is his role to protect his children, to save his children, but their humanity is revealed, and they are saved, only by one who is disgraced. At the end of the day, it is the authoritarian charisma of Atticus—so committed to family and law and, ostensibly, to justice—that blinds him to the humanity of the other.

4

CHARISMA AND TRUTH

From the early days of the Western philosophical tradition, charisma has been opposed to truth. Before Socrates started dialoguing with his fellow citizens in the Athenian marketplace, opinion reigned supreme. The meaning of love, justice, piety, or even truth was determined by the views of the majority. These views were adopted with little reflection, and with little concern for their cogency. Because of this, individuals held various conflicting views, but inconsistency did not concern them. While this might be how all cultures generally treat their beliefs, the power of opinion was particularly strong in Athens because of the privileged role played by persuasion in community life. With direct democracy, it was necessary to persuade fellow citizens of one's point of view if that perspective was to carry the day—to get a new bridge built or to be exonerated of a crime. Language was used to persuade, and an industry of professional persuaders, sophists, gained prominence and wealth. Just as the twenty-four-hour television news cycle morphs how contemporary Americans view current events, and facts about the world more generally, the centrality of persuasion to Athenian life made opinion more important than truth. What mattered was to change opinions by any means necessary; demonstrations of truth were but one such means, and a rather cumbersome one. The paradigmatic way to change opinions was to speak in front of a huge audience, manipulating that audience's desires and emotions so as to sway observers' opinions even if their new opinions ran counter to self-interest. In such performances, reason took a backseat to showmanship and studied rhetoric—to something like charisma.

This world of opinion and persuasion was interrupted by the arrival of Socrates in the Athenian marketplace. Through interrogative dialogues, Socrates would demonstrate the lack of cogency and incoherence of his interlocutors' views about their world and about themselves. He would build on the broadly shared, deep-seated intuition that we ought not to hold contradictory beliefs. Of course we all do, and we happily ignore these contradictions most of the time. Athenian society had become particularly complacent because of the cultural preeminence of persuasion; the virtue of intellectual consistency was desiccating. Socrates did not set out to persuade the masses: this would have put him in competition with the sophists. The role of speaker to the masses was already overdetermined in Athenian society. The orator would have to manipulate the emotions and mute reason or he would be dismissed. Instead, Socrates spoke with his fellow citizens individually. When they attempted to answer at length or with rhetorical flourish, he lost patience, directing them instead to think carefully, to reason. Socrates was searching for truth. He professed ignorance of truth, and he solicited assistance from his interlocutors. This search for truth necessarily began with conventional wisdom, with the opinions of the majority—opinions that sometimes included myth. But it moved from there, through Socrates's probing queries, toward a truth that would never be reached. While the truth Socrates sought would always remain elusive, he and his interlocutors did reach quite decisive conclusions about what was false. Opinions held by the many about justice, love, piety, and much else were false.

Truth, then, must be beyond opinion, even beyond the world, yet Socrates showed that truth is not irrelevant. The affective investment of his interlocutors in the dialectical process, the process of interrogation that Socrates performed, demonstrated the deep desire for truth beyond opinion that characterizes the human. In a sense, it was Socrates even more than the sophists who was attuned to the desires of his audience. Where the sophists sought to fulfill preexisting desires, Socrates stoked a desire that his interlocutors did not even know they had until their encounter with Socrates. This unknown desire grew as reason was employed, not as reason was muted. The more beliefs appeared incoherent through reasoning, the more Socrates's interlocutors desired to know the truth of the matter, the truth about the concept under discussion, and ultimately to know truth itself. Many interlocutors grew frustrated through this process and walked away, turning back to the easy satisfaction offered by the sophists. Their encounters with Socrates did, presumably, leave them with lingering disquietude. The confidence that they once had about how the world fits together and about who they themselves are was shaken. To unsettle individuals, and eventually a whole society, was dangerous. Socrates would ultimately die because of his commitment to truth, quite accurately labeled at his trial as corrupting the youth, worshiping false gods, and introducing a new transcendent. Unlike the sophists, Socrates was not motivated by financial incentives but by a desire he could not ignore, a desire that was contagious—a desire for truth beyond the world.

At first it would seem misleading to label Socrates charismatic. He opposed sophists, such archetypes of greasy charisma that the word continues to be used today. But there is also a sense in which Socrates enchanted those with whom he spoke, and in the *Symposium* and the *Phaedrus* he explicitly describes the role of enchantment, the *daimon* or *eros*, in the pursuit of truth. Socrates must certainly have been thought to possess an extraordinary gift, an ability to shake the confidence of the most self-assured Athenians in their long-held understandings. And he did draw out his listeners' desires, though less to fulfill them than to turn these desires inward, to transform an inarticulate desire into desire to know oneself. Like most charismatics, Socrates must have appeared opaque, an appearance he embraced when he proclaimed his ignorance. The opacity of the sophists, and the sophists of the two and a half millennia that followed, was likely a product of the slickness of their performance, the inescapable intuition, often suppressed, that it must be too slick, that there must be more to the charismatic figure than what meets the eye. Socrates represents democratic charisma, charisma that challenges our view of our self and our world, charisma that refuses to sate our preexisting desires, charisma that short-circuits and so calls attention to all forms of mediation. Socrates was suspicious not only of speaking to crowds but also of written communication: in those forms of communication that he could not short-circuit, he simply refused to participate. When rumor began to overdetermine his image, the only means to short-circuit such mediation was his own death. Yet Socrates was not oblivious to mediation, and he toyed with the materials and forms of the sophists, beginning conversations with conventional wisdom, and, in the *Phaedrus*, he toyed with speech-giving himself in order to show the inadequacy of the medium. The effect of Socrates's democratic charisma was to unsettle. He performed the mystery of his humanity, the inability of his humanity to be reduced to any familiar form of representation, and he encouraged those with whom he spoke to do the same. He encouraged Athenians to challenge the powers that be in Athens, not by attacking the rulers but by attacking the network of ideas, images, and styles of performance that secured the interests of those in power.

Was Martin Luther King, Jr., an avatar of Socrates or a sophist? Certainly his contemporary opponents considered him the latter, and his lackluster performance in traditional debates, when his oratorical gifts were continually undercut by critical questioning, suggests that the association with the sophists might be uncomfortably accurate. After all, King was at his best speaking to large audiences, and his words tapped into the desires of his audience—he was, of course, a preacher. On the other hand, while King may have built on his listeners' preexisting desires for justice or love, the way he used those terms was rather different from conventional wisdom. Many of those who would profess a desire for racial integration in 1975 were appalled at integration two decades earlier, and it is hard to deny that King, or the image of King, had a major role in this change. King was intrigued by philosophy when he studied the subject academically in his youth at the University of Pennsylvania, Boston University, and Harvard. King's most famous text, his letter from a Birmingham jail, refers explicitly to Socrates as offering a model to be emulated in the civil rights movement. Socrates believed "it was necessary to create a tension in the mind so that individuals could rise from the bondage of myths and half truths," and King's mode of protest was intent on creating such tension. In his sermons and lectures, King repeatedly invoked world-transcending truth to which we aspire through reflection and action. Yet King himself was not always an exemplary figure of integrity, with his vast plagiarism and duplicitous romantic life. Moreover, whatever democratic charisma

King himself may have at first possessed in those early days of a local bus boycott in Alabama, the huge media attention he attracted made it exceedingly difficult for his charisma to remain democratic.

This tension between King's association with Socrates and his association with the sophists is at the center of Charles Johnson's novel *Dreamer*, published in 1998. While Johnson's work of historical fiction is not a masterpiece—though it is good enough that its lack of greatness can be frustrating—*Dreamer* offers an opening to reflect on King's charisma that cuts through the charismatic veneer so often the focus of both the champions and the critics of King's charisma. The book's title signals this alternative focus. King is to be represented as a dreamer rather than a preacher. In one sense, this shifts the focus to King's inner life and away from his famed performances. However, King's most famous performance is abbreviated as his "dream"—"I have a dream." This dream is so often understood as a metaphor, representing a collective hope for the future, that Johnson's title startles by pointing to a human being who dreams. The one-word title encapsulates a theory of charisma by linking King's familiar, outward performance of charisma with his often-forgotten inner life. That inner life should not be erased by a focus on dazzling oratorical performance, the title argues; that performance is dependent on and produced by King accessing and mobilizing his inwardness.

Dreamer does not simply humanize King by, for example, providing imagined behind-the-scenes access to the larger-than-life man. Such an approach would make King familiar by making him similar to the humans who we know. But such an approach can only humanize in the most superficial sense, for it can only describe humans in the same way that animals, objects, and even concepts are described—enumerating their features, recording events that transpire. Even if the description of an individual involves what we take to be particularly human, such as reasoning and emotion, these are still presented as predicates attached to subjects, offering the reader a sense of understanding. The reader would leave with the confidence that *these* are the salient features of so-and-so. If the reader were to meet so-and-so, she would feel as if they are already acquainted; she would not be surprised at whom she sees. But if the human marks a knot in our representations of the world, ungraspable and always surprising, presenting an individual through a list of their primary characteristics is essentially dehumanizing. How is the unrepresentable to be represented? That is the challenge, and magic, of charisma, but it is also the challenge of literature. Mediocre literature assures us that we know the world, even as it may entertain; good literature opens us to the surprises of the world. Words come together in unexpected ways, characters grapple with tragic choices, and the reader's expectations are thwarted without losing the reader's attention.

This is Johnson's aspiration in *Dreamer*: to present a fictionalized King who intrigues for more than voyeuristic reasons, to create a character who does more than satisfy the reader's preexisting desires. One approach would be to craft a King character with impenetrable depths, a character whose representation always hints at the presence of more that goes unrepresented. For a character whose image is so overdetermined by readers' preconceptions and media representations, this approach would be difficult if not impossible to employ successfully. Every hint at the unrepresented would be immediately taken as a pointer to the reader's own preexisting knowledge of King. Johnson tries another approach: he creates two Kings. At the center of the novel's plot is the appearance and development of King's body double, a character named Chaym Smith. The two men, King

and Smith, share a striking resemblance but have quite different personalities and life histories. King's background was relatively privileged for a black man in the South; Smith was among
the lowliest of the low, leading a life full of deprivations in the
North. As the novel proceeds, the two men increasingly blend
into each other and are confused for each other; it becomes
clear that they were never as different as it had seemed. However, they remain two: there are two Kings in one. Johnson
leverages a powerful intuition about the impossibility of representing the human: two individuals are always distinct no matter
how many outward qualities they share. If humans were reducible to lists of their qualities, two people with the same list would
be entirely indistinguishable. We know this is not so—and so
we are continually reminded that there is more to King than we
can grasp, more to King than Johnson could represent. Even as
the characters blend, our instinct is to resist assimilation, to attempt to discern when it is King speaking and when it is Smith.
If the reader does allow herself to let the two characters become
one, she must accept that one individual, King, can contain
within himself irreconcilable differences. The backgrounds and
personalities of Smith and King are so different that any attempt
to comfortably grasp the man, King, is thwarted by the knowledge that he cannot be both *this* and *that*.

   In addition to the pairing of Smith and King that drives the
narrative, *Dreamer* also is structured around another, more subtle pairing. The book's narrator (alternate chapters are in the
first person), Matthew, is an anonymous volunteer with King's
Southern Christian Leadership Conference. Matthew is tasked
with preparing Smith to impersonate King. Where King is a
national leader, Matthew is an anonymous supporter, but the
two men are portrayed as having certain significant similari-
ties. In his youth, King was "a shy, bookish man who went to

great lengths not to call unnecessary attention to himself" (25). Despite these inclinations, King had a gift for public speaking and gained prominence. Matthew has no such gift and remains bookish and solitary. In the performance of the novel, however, Matthew does have a gift: the ability to write, to narrate. Here Johnson associates the charisma of the speaker with the charisma-like skill of the writer, each a thoughtful, guarded individual struggling to express his humanity in a mediated way. As Johnson portrays it, King and Matthew share an interest in reading, particularly in philosophy. In their one extended conversation, they discuss Nietzsche, who Matthew finds intriguing but who King warns against. Matthew explores the world of ideas and explores his self, largely alone, while King reminisces of the days when he was able to do the same, the days before his schedule was packed with speeches and interviews. In this dou-bling, of the narrator and King, the novel hints at the possibility that King himself could be its author, reflecting on the com-plexities of his self and performing in writing a depth of charac-ter that he is unable to perform in front of the microphones and cameras.

That King has a special gift, from God, is clearly affirmed by *Dreamer*, yet this gift is not identified with King's charisma. The gift King has is a natural talent, or a supernatural talent; King's charisma is something more. When the novel opens, in Chicago during the later, less successful, less glamorous phase of King's public career, King is burdened by this divine gift. He understands himself to be called to do God's work, but this is not easy. Black Americans are viewing King as a saint, living a life committed to truth, but King feels himself to be an ordi-nary human being employed by God to advance justice. The oratorical gift he is given from above brings with it the duty to use it serving God's purposes; from the outside King may look like a saint but King himself is a weary mortal. Johnson evocatively captures this burdened gift when he describes the knife wound that King received shortly after the successful Montgomery bus boycott. A crazed woman stabbed King and he almost died, but the doctors were able to repair the wound—in the process carving a cross in his chest. For the rest of his life King would carry the scars of this cross, the gift of medical salvation standing in for, and identified with, the divine gift King was to employ for the nation's salvation. Both were imposed on a mortal body, a body always under threat of death, and both suggest that King's life was encumbered by the salvific gift. People may confuse King with a god, placing a portrait of the black leader next to their portrait of Jesus, but King is no god. He is faced with an acute, and universal, challenge: to recognize his mortality and humanity while also realizing his talents, really, to express his humanity through his talents. Cultivating a talent too often means embracing the ways of the world at the expense of the self: mastering the norms of a practice fueled by the recognition that one receives. To be excellent at a social practice means ceding one's self to the norms of that practice; yet the self cannot be expressed except through social practice. This is the problem posed by King's charisma and by charisma in general, but it is also the challenge of being human.

As *Dreamer* portrays it, King is losing his humanity by the time he reaches Chicago. In his youth, he enjoyed reading philosophy, teaching Greek, and quoting Socrates. This world of intellectual engagement and self-discovery that took the young Southerner to the academic and cultural centers of the North is now in his past. King is overdetermined by his image, and this takes away his humanity. The movement of which he is a leader has a life of its own, and he has become an instrument of that movement. "It was no longer his life to do with as he pleased,"

Johnson writes. "As it is with candles, so it was with him: the more light he gave, the less there was of him" (14–15). The visual imagery here is significant: like the idol that captures and holds the gaze, skewing perception and judgment, King's image was magnified and attracted the gaze of onlookers. To capture their gaze, he fulfilled their desires, desires that were in part shaped by the framing of King as a redemptive figure. Each time he was represented in the media, regardless of what he was saying or doing, the desires of viewers were stoked further, and these desires would be fulfilled and again stoked by the next media appearance. Even if each time he appeared before the cameras King would tell viewers to focus on the movement rather than on an individual, this would not be heard. The eyes would close the ears. It was only King as image that mattered—there was no space left for King the human. King himself could not engage responsively with the world because the world would not respond to him: the world would only respond to the image of King, the King who was inhuman. Even away from the Southern scenery that usually surrounded him, even as he lived in the Chicago ghetto, King could not escape his mediated double; they had become almost entirely one and the same.

Johnson vividly describes how King was almost lost in his own image. "More than any place else, [King] was at home there, in the pulpit, leaning into the microphones" (136). King's gift of oratory, given by God and channeling God, was no longer possessed by King; it *was* King. This gift was not only preaching ability, it was highly mediated preaching: it was preaching into microphones, tape recorders, video cameras, and reporters' notebooks. This had become King's "home," the place where he felt comfortable, the place where he felt most himself. He felt comfortable where he was his image. As Johnson tells it, this was not always the case. In his youth, "His public self had seemed so different to him, like a mask; but then he realized some few years later that man and mask were fused" (137–138). Johnson is equivocal on the cause of this fusion. While he writes that it was "the Movement" that was its cause, Johnson's descriptions of King suggest that it was the technologies of mediation that caused it. It is tempting to imagine a social movement in a less media-saturated age that allowed time and space for its most prominent figures to be genuinely off-stage. Yet this does not seem quite right: the imagination, fueled by second- and thirdhand accounts of a charismatic leader, is likely just as powerful at overdetermining the image of that leader as television cameras and tweets, if not more so. The apparently unmediated leader also struggles to remain responsive to the world because she is likewise fixed in the images of her interlocutors. The problem is not so much with media as it is with the dominant trope of the social movement that necessarily involves a leader, discounting the agency and wisdom of a movement's many participants. It is this trope that feeds and is fed by media, dehumanizing King. As Johnson portrays it, King's humanity is so stripped by this process that it leads to his death. The everyman narrator, Matthew, concludes the book by stating that he knows who killed King: "We all did" (235). In a sense, King had already died: stripped of his humanity, he was a story arc that needed to conclude. Indeed, Matthew himself, as narrator, is particularly complicit in this murder: he is the one telling the story, adding yet one more layer onto the overdetermination of King's image.

While Johnson laments the foreclosure of King's humanity, he is careful to indicate that a trace of this humanity always remains. On Johnson's telling, King has a "deeper, esoteric message about freedom" that he was unable to convey (17). It is at this point, when Johnson marks a trace of the human that remains, that Johnson introduces the character of King's double. It is through this double, it would seem, that the esoteric message brought by King can be developed—in two senses: by King himself, because the double will allow King time away from the world of mediation, and by Johnson in the performance of his narrative. Something else is happening when King's double enters the picture. The world is falling apart. There is violence, chaos, and mayhem in the streets of Chicago as morally driven, nonviolent confrontation with racism is met with violent resistance by white Chicagoans. As King's own humanity is foreclosed, the humanity of the world, or at least the city, is also foreclosed, with whites treating blacks as animals to be controlled and so degrading themselves to less-than-human status as instruments of control. King is frustrated, seemingly helpless. Then Chaym Smith enters.

Chaym is the Hebrew word for life, and the entrance of Chaym Smith brings life back to King, and back to the world of the novel. They are very different men, but they quickly begin to become one. Upon meeting, their breath synchronizes. They look essentially the same, though not identical. As they talk, the different paths their lives have taken become clear. Smith has faced a series of broken relationships, debilitating poverty, and white cruelty. Where King came from a line of respectable black preachers, Smith's parentage is misty and his lumpen self-presentation reminds King of the white image of blacks he was trying to break. The combination of resemblance and difference quickly causes King unease. As Johnson narrates, rather heavy-handedly, King suddenly worries that his commitment to equality was misplaced. How could King ask that he and Smith be treated as equals, given their vast differences? King was talented and well bred; Smith was apparently a talentless bastard. Johnson has King reaffirm his commitment to equality, but now with more nuance: "Despite the fortuitous differences in men, they could volunteer to share one another's fate" (49). Even though Smith was lower than King, King could identify with Smith in the struggle for racial equality. But Johnson's text offers a more compelling possibility. Rather than acknowledging human difference while still affirming racial equality, the text is suggesting that we refine our view of the human. It is not social status, upbringing, or lineage that defines the human, but that which exceeds all such descriptions, all that is representable. Smith poses a challenge to King's politics of respectability—the way King leverages his educated vocabulary, his family connections, and his suits—in a way that shifts the political conversation away from equality. The language of equality could just as easily be applied to plants or rocks as it could be to people; it ignores our humanity. When it is this humanity, exceeding our ability to represent, that is at issue, something closer to the language of dignity seems apt. Dignity suggests that there is some quality of each human being that cannot be quantified or represented but that must not be violated. There is something to human life that escapes the grasp of political calculation. This is what the name Chaym Smith suggests: Smith points to the utterly ordinary, the anonymous, while Chaym points to the essence of life. By encountering Chaym Smith, King sees that the struggle he is waging is to protect the dignity of each human being rather than to advance an abstract principle of equality. Put another way, in the mediated world where King was identified with his image, it was the play of concepts, like equality, that mattered. When he encounters irresistible evidence for the human, exceeding representation, the hold of political rhetoric breaks as he sees the human itself—in another and in himself.

It is not only Smith's name that points to the way he represents the human. When Smith first arrives in the circle of

King's associates, he wears a "faint smile on his lips . . . as if he carried unsayable secrets (or sins)" (33). The way Smith carries himself suggests that there is more to him than one would think. It is not that he looks like a deep or profound person. Rather, his appearance is opaque: it suggests that quick conclusions should not be drawn from that appearance. His appearance suggests that he has experienced much in life, but that these experiences would not be captured by historiography. In this sense, Smith is exactly the inverse of King. The latter is known to all through his representation, yet all also implicitly know that the man must be more than this representation. Smith seems unknowable to all, essentially opaque, yet at the same time we know that he is not wholly alien. Smith's opacity extends beyond his appearance. His language itself is hard to pin down. Sometimes he uses black vernacular as if he were on a South Side street corner, at other times he speaks in perfect standard English. This opacity is described at some points in the novel as acting or mimicry. It would seem as though Smith, the everyman, can become any man, adopting the languages he hears and the self-performances he sees. This, it appears at first, is why Smith is essentially opaque: he is nothing more than what he hears around him. Perhaps he had once had a fixed identity—"I always wanted to preach" (35), he says—but his life kept hitting rough patches preventing him from embracing that vocation. Now he wanders. In other words, Smith poses a challenge for accounts of the human as that which exceeds representation, a sophistic challenge. He seems to exceed representation not because of his humanity but precisely because of his lack of humanity, because he has become the conduit for the words of others with no principled commitments of his own. Smith imitates others to further his self-interest, cleverly: the novel's narrator describes him as "Machiavellian." He seems aligned with the sophists. From this perspective, King seems to be Socrates, committed to the truth unto death and using his talents to persuade others to share this commitment.

Indeed, Smith saw in King something he was lacking, and something he wanted. Smith, the narrator Matthew tells us, "was determined to *possess* the mystery of the minister's power and popularity, to make it his own," a mystery that Smith elsewhere refers to as the secret to "Immortality" (102, 43). Smith and King could recognize in each other that which exceeds representation, but in King this "mystery" attracts a following whereas Smith's life was a series of misadventures. Smith is convinced that King's mystery must have substance; he is convinced that, in contrast, at his own core he has "just emptiness" (86). Smith rejects all forms of representation as lies, asserting, "As soon as you squeeze experience into a sentence—or a story—it's suspect" (92). He tells the narrator that it is necessary to move beyond such falsehoods. When Matthew asks what, precisely, this advice means, Smith responds that he is not sure, that he is still investigating. Where King would access truth through representation, through colorful and gripping oratory, Smith found in such oratory only deceit, used to advance the interests of the orator. The only thing we can be confident about is the truth of biological life, Smith seems to suggest. While he is decrying representation he is sitting in a latrine, "emptying his bowels loudly, with trumpeting flatulence and gurgling sounds and a stink so mephitic it made me choke" (93).

Smith's lowly status naturally brings with it rough manners. We are told of his various noisy bodily processes. But as the narrative progresses Johnson begins to describe King similarly: he belches, food sticks in his teeth. King is supposed to be the one swimming in a world of lofty ideas, but we soon find that Smith himself has read widely and enjoys intellectual engagement, though without pretense about its significance. Both King and Smith have eclectic intellectual tastes, with a particular interest in religious wisdom from the East. Before their meeting, Smith was, of course, aware of their resemblance. He would clip newspaper articles that tarnished King. More precisely, they tarnished King's image, reminding their readers, and particularly Smith, that King was ultimately an ordinary human being with ordinary virtues and vices. Matthew, the narrator, is puzzled by Smith's habit. It was "as if he took a delicious pleasure in publicity that diminished the man he so resembled and clearly revered" (59). Smith's fundamental commitment is to the humanity of all, a humanity that exceeds representation, and this is a humanity shared by King and him, despite media-fueled appearances to the contrary. Indeed, both Smith and King are entranced by the other, not so much because of a narcissistic pleasure in identification with the self as because of the ease with which they are able to clearly see humanity itself. When looking at anyone else, they would have to cut through the sedimented habits and practices and physical appearance to find that humanity, to find the human. When looking at themselves they are distracted by their own habits of self-representation even as they intuit that these are inadequate. But it is when looking at the other who is both the same and different, sharing outward appearances but thwarting the desire to represent the other as the self, that it is crystal-clear that something ineffable is encountered: the human.

Smith and King are physically nearly identical, but they have one crucial, distinguishing physical difference. Smith has a crippled leg. It is hard to avoid the phallic significance of the crippled leg. King has a strong father and children of his own, and he has a healthy leg. He transmits the best of black culture and religion from generation to generation. Smith does not know his father and has no children; he is outside the heteronormative logic that attributes strength to reproduction. In the way the novel is framed, Johnson is challenging the identification of the strong leg, the phallus, the family, with charisma—or at least with democratic charisma. King has strong legs but, in Chicago, he is incapacitated. His efforts to achieve social justice are going nowhere; the world is descending into chaos. The problem, the novel suggests, is not charisma; the problem is the identification of charisma with the phallus. This identification makes charisma authoritarian, not democratic—and it ultimately makes charisma ineffectual. What the novel seems to be suggesting is that King needs to recognize that charisma does not require the phallus—put another way, that the human is not the male. With this recognition, with this assimilation of Smith into himself, King can exercise democratic charisma.

The way that Johnson describes King—or is it Smith?— speaking to a church audience in the one substantial description of oratorical performance in *Dreamer* sounds like a paradigm of democratic charisma. The preacher was "speaking to all gathered, yes, but in a way not to us at all—or, more exactly, to the spirit immanent in each parishioner, offering his speech as a form of sacrifice, holding nothing back, forgetting himself utterly in the demands of the moment and allowing the Father within him to doeth the work and the Father within us to receive it" (140). Democratic charisma does not offer the same product to each consumer, satisfying preexisting, culturally constituted desires. Democratic charisma speaks to each individual, challenging listeners to interrogate themselves, stoking the desire for such self-interrogation, the capacity that marks our humanity. We know that we are more than we seem, more than the world makes us seem, but we often forget; the preacher exercising democratic charisma reminds us. In other words, democratic charisma speaks to the humanity of each and calls forth that humanity. Johnson uses theological language here: the humanity called forth is "spirit," that which is perpendicular to the concerns of the world is "the Father." The charismatic speaker does not display herself but rather challenges the world's conception of itself by calling on that which is perpendicular to the world, that which is illegible in worldly terms: "the Father." Note that there is no content to "the Father" here beyond His otherness; He simply marks that which thwarts the world's efforts at representation—which is to say, He simply represents our humanity. If the speaker were to hold something back or to remember herself during her performance, this would mean remaining invested in the ways of the world, in the terms the world gives us to see ourselves. Charisma is contagious. The more the humanity of the speaker is drawn out, the more the humanity in the listeners is drawn out: "the Father within him" brings out the same "Father within us." It is particularly significant that the narrator, Matthew, has difficulty discerning whether it is Smith or King preaching. After all, it is the Smith in King, as it were, that makes King such a compelling speaker. It is the ordinary life possessed by all that is harnessed by King in his most charismatic performances. It is this life (*chaym*) that is on display, this life that remains when all our attributes are stripped away—this life that images, or is, the Father.

Shortly after he is introduced in the novel, Smith displays his mangled leg to the narrator. He then looks at Matthew, the anonymous everyman, "flashing that ironical, almost erotic smirk again, as if somehow we were co-conspirators, or maybe he knew something scandalous about me, though we'd met only minutes earlier" (35). Smith is unencumbered by an identification of phallus with self: he knows he is still human despite having a mangled leg. He shows his humanity to Matthew, knowing

that it will stoke Matthew's desire—because he knows that
Matthew, too, beneath it all, is human, "something scandalous"
but not expressible. Smith has charisma: he intrigues and attracts Matthew no matter how much Matthew, invested in the
respectability politics of the Southern Christian Leadership
Conference, would like to resist that attraction. Smith's charisma is presented at first as Socratic: he does not make long
speeches, everything he says seems ironic, and he always begins
with the everyday, never with lofty ideals. He converses individually with Matthew and, sometimes, with Matthew's coworker, Amy. Smith starts where they are, with the ideas they
have, and pushes them to think more critically. He embraces
his ignorance: it is the only thing to which he is clearly committed. "Who *are* you?" Matthew asks him. "I dunno . . . I'm always findin' that out. I guess I make it up as I go along. Pull off
there, I got to pee" (67). Smith has an imaginative, or at least
imitative, spirit that pushes beyond the purely negative, critical
dimension of Socrates—a spirit perhaps at home in the reverie
of the *Symposium*. Note also the disidentification of the critical
spirit Smith cultivates and the phallus: this profession of ignorance
is juxtaposed with a desire to urinate rather than to procreate.
Indeed, unlike Socrates, Smith never rises from the earthly to
the lofty realm of Ideas. Such an ascent would conceal the human; Smith never departs from what is most basically human.

Matthew recognizes the echoes of Socrates in both King
and Smith. He recalls King telling him, "Son, the best thing
you can do is try to understand yourself," and he reflects that
this is precisely what Smith has prompted him to work at (85).
But note how, in King's advice, Matthew is already interpellated.
He is already "son," the son of King, part of a lineage, child
of the fecund charismatic. King is not urging Matthew to
know himself in the abstract, but to know himself in context,

situated in a tradition, part of a community. Smith's critical self-interrogation begins from nowhere, questions everything at once, and never reaches a conclusion, no matter how provisional.

When asked another time, by a minister, whether he is Christian, Smith responds, "The truth is, I don't know what I am, and I like it that way. Leaves me lots of room to be surprised every day" (158). Smith here is concerned with truth, even if he seems to use the word flippantly. The truth that Smith affirms is human ignorance, the limitations of the human, and the need to embrace those limitations. Rather than attempting to get the world right, he urges that we allow ourselves to be surprised, and this is only possible when we recognize the limitations of the labels that the world assigns to us. This is freedom, according to Smith's statements and performances. But Smith is mindful that this freedom occurs in a context not only of enforced social norms but also of systematic discrimination and inequities. He was kicked out of a monastery in Japan for being a foreigner, and he realizes he cannot be at home anywhere, even in his homeland. "Wherever I go, I'm a nigger" (158). In a sense, Smith is arguing that blacks, and particularly poor blacks, have special access to their humanity. When the laws and customs of the world are against you, it is easier to loosen yourself from the world's hold, to realize that you are more than the world says that you are. Smith is rejected everywhere he goes, and this continually reinforces his view that the ways of the world are amiss, that he must stand apart from them.

After things go wrong in Chicago, Smith travels with Matthew and Amy to rural Illinois, where they had prepared him for his job as King's double. There, Smith works as a church groundskeeper. This creates a stark juxtaposition between King the preacher and Smith the groundskeeper. The two men depend on each other, need each other for their success, but their paths only coincide briefly—they coincide for the speech described earlier that so clearly exemplifies democratic charisma. King goes back to his life immersed in, and drowned by, the media spotlight; Smith remains on the periphery. Apart, democratic charisma is absent. King needs Smith's humanity, but Smith also needs something. He may seem content on the margins, but something is amiss. Eventually, when confronted by federal agents who want his services and who threaten to charge him with offenses from his youth, Smith accepts their offer. Unlike Socrates, Smith in his commitment to interrogating his own ignorance is not accompanied by a commitment to the good. Not knowing who he is leads Smith to float wherever the winds may take him. The winds took him to King, and they take him to the federal agents. Smith's apparent charisma turns out to be sophistry, language that entertains while advancing self-interest. Smith needs King because Smith needs mediation. He needs to recognize the cultural substance in which he was formed and in which he lives. Smith knows he is more than what the world says about him, but he takes this as a license to ignore the ways of the world. He forgets, or never knows, that his humanity can only be accessed through appreciating and short-circuiting those ways of the world. Smith senses this superficially: he is clever, he has a way with words. But he has not mastered the media in the way that King has, with a deep understanding of cultural practices of black and white worlds as well as an appreciation for the technologies through which culture circulates.

In short, Smith lacks the virtue of charisma. The result is the simulacrum of democratic charisma, that is, authoritarian charisma, which is not a virtue at all. Smith dominates the lives of those around him—Matthew, Amy—without any respect for their dignity, for the human in them. He feeds their desire in the same way that King feeds their desire, giving them what they want, even when what they want is a feeling of self-sacrifice. Near the end of the novel, after Smith has gone away with the federal agents, Amy asks Matthew where Smith might be. "I thought hard. 'Everywhere . . .'" (236). Matthew concludes that everyone killed King by foreclosing King's humanity, and he concludes that Smith is everywhere because humanity is to be found everywhere. The problem—that is solved by the virtue of charisma—is to allow the humanity of Smith to show itself without being captured in an image, like the image of King. When Smith laments, "Shit, as long as *he's* alive, I guess I'll always be nothing," what he is saying is that the image of himself, himself as King, as media-managed King, takes away the opportunity for Smith to be human (130). Here Johnson is pointing toward the fundamental challenge posed by *Dreamer*, that mediation takes away humanity but is also necessary to be human, and Johnson also points toward the solution. He has written a book about charisma to solve this dilemma, a book that shows how charisma can be democratic but also how democratic charisma so easily slips away.

While the pairing of King and Smith is at the heart of *Dreamer* and performs the book's central argument about charisma, this argument is repeated and enriched in the portrayal of the narrator, Matthew. At the beginning of the novel, Matthew declares, "I was nobody," "a nothing," "a cog in a vast machine" (26). Through the telling of the story, through the writing of the book, Matthew finds his humanity. This dynamic illustrates the contagion of charisma, the way charisma spreads from charismatic figures, King/Smith, to those who witness them. As King and Smith probe their humanity through their encounter, Matthew, as witness, is prompted to explore his own humanity—and produce his own charismatic precipitate, the novel itself.

Crucially, King alone is incapable of eliciting such a response from Matthew. The machine in which Matthew feels himself a cog is, in fact, the civil rights movement; he is a full-time movement volunteer. As the novel opens, King's charisma is authoritarian, simply advancing the goals of an organization by appealing to the preexisting desires of listeners. King can do little more because of the media overdetermination of his image. Even though King represents manliness, with his respected lineage and fully functioning legs, King is impotent when it comes to calling forth the humanity of his followers, including of Matthew. Listeners may respond to King, but their response is essentially passive. When Smith enters the picture, Matthew has an immediate, "erotic" response. Soon, when confronted with a racist waitress, Matthew abandons his superficially professed nonviolence and hurls a hamburger at the waitress.

At first, Smith arouses and angers Matthew. Then, as Smith and King converge toward a figure of democratic charisma, this charisma becomes contagious. At the novel's start, Matthew is a loner, frequently rejected by women. Amy, Matthew's coworker who shares with him the task of training Smith, also rejects his advances. She is too drawn to the phallic charisma of King: "I need somebody a little more like the men I knew when I was growing up. Or like Dr. King" (94). The clear replacement of her father with King as object of sexual desire sidelines the fatherless, childless Matthew. After some time with Smith, things begin to change. When Amy grows frustrated with Smith and returns to Chicago, she suggests that she and Matthew might go out when he returns to the city. He returns and calls her, and she suggests that they go on a date to a black nationalist's lecture. Amy's and Matthew's allegiances are still too tied to the nonviolence and spirituality of King; they argue with the militant speaker and eventually leave, frustrated.

Black nationalism performs authoritarian charisma at its worst, Johnson is suggesting (though the author seems to forget that black nationalists certainly face the same challenges of media overdetermination that he so vividly depicts in the case of King). From the novel's perspective, and from Amy's, militant rhetoric is ultimately impotent, or counterproductive. She longs for the fulfillment she expects from a charismatic leader, and now she believes it can be found with Matthew. Amy invites him back to her apartment, tells him she feels "soiled," and invites him to shower with her. Authoritarian charisma violates: it offers easy fulfillment of desires in order to achieve its ends, getting what it wants from an audience treated as less than human. Matthew, now infected with democratic charisma, offers something different. He is now potent, but he is not overbearing. He offers the possibility of love rather than lust, of a cleansing shower together.

This was the potential on offer in the relationship between Amy and Matthew, but it was potential that went unrealized. Amy had not broken free of authoritarian charisma's spell. She was looking for a better father—going from her job working with King to the black nationalist's lecture and then to Matthew. She desires Matthew not because of who he is, or because of the ways she can grow with him, but because of how he will give her what she wants. She thought King or the black nationalist would give her what she wanted, but each left her unfulfilled and frustrated; each wanted something from her. In contrast, Matthew asks nothing of her and tries to fully please her. As he, in his narrator's voice, recounts, "I said, *Tell me what you want me to do*, which she did, and for the next two hours—or perhaps it was three—I did everything Amy wanted, in just the way she wanted it" (177–178, italics in original). They would have gone on for hours more, except they are interrupted by a phone call from Smith. He and King have parted ways, and each has moved away from their momentary union in democratic charisma. Smith needs Matthew, and Matthew leaves his tryst immediately. At the end of the day, it only seemed as if he had been infected by democratic charisma. In fact, he had not interrogated his humanity, and he had not embarked on a quest for truth. He remained an object utilized by those around him, subject to the power of the substitute father's phallus.

Johnson's *Dreamer* does not settle the question of whether King should be aligned with Socrates or the sophists. Rather, it reframes the question, emphasizing the precariousness of the search for truth—which is to say, the precariousness of democratic charisma, and the precariousness of the human. It is much easier, and more comfortable, to embrace the authoritarian charisma of the father, or of father substitutes, than it is to witness or perform democratic charisma. Between the pull of alienation and the pull of mediation, it is difficult to reach a sustainable balance. Rather than looking for this balance in one of Johnson's characters, perhaps it makes sense to find it performed in the text itself, to read the novel as a democratic-charismatic performance. Mediation is inescapable in literature, but literature at its best challenges the omnipotence of mediation, challenges the reader to approach self and world differently, more critically. Johnson approaches this task head-on, by taking as his protagonists paradigms of authoritarian charisma and narrating the possibilities through which their authoritarianism can be mitigated or challenged. Democratic charisma does not provide an answer, does not speak the Truth. Democratic charisma performs truthfully, teaching lessons in critique and calling on an audience to join in.

5

CHARISMA AND BEAUTY

S ocrates was ugly, or so the tradition says. His charisma was not in spite of his ugliness, it was because of it. The dissonance between physical appearance and oratorical or dialectical performance reminds listeners of the humanity of the performer and so calls attention to the contingency of the performance. The ideas communicated may be powerful, and they may be important, but they are coming from *this* human being, *here*. Indeed, this particular human being is more important to the charismatic performance than the ideas communicated: it is his or her humanity that is revealed in charismatic performances, at their best. We are reminded that the speaker is more than she seems, that neither an elegant appearance nor a gifted tongue should lead us to believe that we know who the speaker is; her performance demonstrates that who she is exceeds any account of what she is. Does this mean that charismatic performers, or charismatic performances, are necessarily ugly? Quite to the contrary: they are necessarily beautiful. Beauty takes us beyond ourselves, beyond the ways we have usually seen ourselves and our worlds, providing an occasion to see differently and to act differently. *Beauty* is often used in a more mundane sense to mean nice-looking or attractive to the eye. Socrates was not this, so he was ugly. Just as excellence means more than following established rules or norms exceedingly well, beauty means more than successfully attracting attention and offering visual pleasure. The more mundane sense of beauty is often paired with the more mundane sense of charisma: If charisma in this superficial sense, authoritarian charisma, fulfills the preexisting desires of an audience, it is clear how it must be beautiful in this more mundane sense, fulfilling an audience's desire for that which is easy on the eye, or the ear. Democratic charisma, the charisma of Socrates, is not beautiful in this superficial sense. The initial reaction to such charisma is often frustration rather than immediate pleasure. But taken as a whole, as a performance rather than as a particular word or gesture, democratic charisma is beautiful. Socrates's physical appearance may be ugly, but Socrates the charismatic is beautiful.

While some have theorized ugliness to mean asymmetry or incoherence, this is clearly not the case. There can be beauty in asymmetry and incoherence, beauty that is achieved when that asymmetry or incoherence is understood against a broader background. This is what superficial accounts of ugliness and beauty so frequently miss: that our judgments of beauty are not judgments of a particular component of a work, nor are they judgments of all of the components of the work. They are judgments of a work in relationship with the cultural substance against which the work is arrayed, to which it necessarily makes reference. The components are not enough, and the work as a whole is not enough: it is the work in relation to that cultural substance, which is to say, those networks of mediation, that matters in making a work beautiful, or ugly. Components of a beautiful work can be ugly, and all the components taken together can be ugly, but when those components, together as a work, are viewed within a cultural context, they can be beautiful. Anger can be beautiful, the grotesque can be beautiful, sadness can be beautiful, and waste can be beautiful (as the huge Internet traffic attracted by pictures of abandoned cars and shopping malls attests). This cultural substance is, specifically, the repertoire of words, images, performances, and technologies that allow for communication in a community and give that community the color and rhythm of its world, as it were. Beauty is inseparable from mediation, but beauty also marks the limits of mediation. To be beautiful is to pull the observer momentarily above that mediated world, to remind the viewer that mediation is not all there is, that it does not make me all of who I am. Beauty hints at that excess by leveraging mediation—and this is exactly what charisma at its best does as well.

To consider the beauty of charisma is to push against the tendency to approach charisma, and much else, by flattening it into culture. So flattened, charisma is descriptive, one cultural practice among many, perhaps linked to other cultural practices that may be deemed problematic or beneficial. These last terms of judgment may sound normative, but they are judgments of practical rationality: some cultural practices are useful for attaining certain desirable ends, others are not, but those ends are never not put in question, and they are assumed to be suspiciously close to personal preference. Seriously asking questions about beauty means refusing the reduction of charisma to a cultural practice. It means allowing for the possibility that charisma can challenge cultural practices, that charisma speaks to part of our humanity not reducible to our culture. If charisma is understood in this way, it requires critical judgment—precisely in the way that beauty requires critical judgment. Art works and performances that are not beautiful may seem beautiful; in time, as individual and collective judgment refines, as our appreciation of the work and its cultural backdrop sharpens, it becomes clear that our judgment was erroneous. This is the challenge in rightly identifying charisma: authoritarian charisma may seem democratic to many. Sharpened judgment and experience will reveal the error; experiencing democratic charisma sharpens judgment and offers experience.

All this should not be taken to suggest that beauty and charisma are one and the same. *Beauty* is a term applied broadly, to the human, to human creations, and to the natural world. Democratic charisma is beautiful, but beauty is not necessarily charismatic. Even human beauty is not necessarily charismatic: a beautiful body or a beautiful speech may pull us outside our ordinary way of seeing the world, may allow us to see ourselves differently, but may not tell us anything about what it means to be human. Charisma performs humanity. It invites viewers to examine their humanity by performing humanity. Such a performance is necessarily beautiful because the human is beautiful. Indeed, the human is beauty itself, for the human is nothing more than a site where cultural substance is incomplete, and so is short-circuited, allowing us both to see vividly and newly that cultural substance and to see how it is crucially limited. All other forms of beauty do this only indirectly and limitedly, drawing on specific cultural practices to allow us to put others in relief; charisma deals with culture as a whole.

If charisma displays what is essentially human, beyond cultural inessentials, it would seem as though someone who has lost his or her culture would be particularly charismatic. This might direct us toward exile or alienation, but an even more profound sense of loss is involved when a culture itself vanishes, leaving its remaining members bare, stripped of their repertoire of language, images, stories, and practices, left with just themselves. The paradigm, here, is indigenous people whose cultures have largely vanished. The vocabularies, images, and concepts that once made possible social practices are gone; cultural substance is gone. There is, indeed, a trope of the wise, lonely Indian watching his or her way of life disappear, but possessing a quiet, unmistakable charisma (just as there is a mystique rather like charisma that surrounds exiles and the alienated). Such charisma is authoritarian rather than democratic. It overdetermines the charismatic individual by identifying her with her (receding or lost) culture, imagined as alien to the dominant culture, that is, the culture where the charisma is witnessed. Moreover, stripped of culture, there are no resources for critical interrogation of self and world—this requires mediation. Without such resources, what is left is an embrace of the self that is imagined by others, or fantasized by others. This self is constituted by nostalgia, the substance of culture condensed into a memory of a lost past both in the minds of the survivors and in the minds of those from the dominant culture who watch them. Charisma depends on mediation, but the American Indian, for example, is imagined to be part of an alien world, a world where there once was mediation but it is no more. The imagined gap between lost, other culture and dominant culture erases the possibility of mediation—even as there is, quite obviously and necessarily, mediation. There is communication, there is perception, there is responsiveness; there are shared languages and images and performances, but these are elided by the perceived cultural difference, ensuring that the charisma of the cultural other is authoritarian. In this case, the word *authoritarian* points to the authority of the dominant culture that is enforced by the perceived charisma of the other, authority that is confirmed by the implicit elimination of the authority of the lost culture. It once had authority, but now that is in the past, marked by the charisma of the Indian elder and his antiquated accoutrements— its authority is no more.

Sherman Alexie's *Reservation Blues* is the story of the ambivalence of charisma amid cultural devastation. With a huge amount of cultural substance destroyed, Alexie holds nonetheless that democratic charisma is possible. It is possible once we recognize the forms of mediation—languages, genres, art forms, technologies—that are shared between dominant and devastated culture. Specifically, Alexie explores the democratic potential in the charisma of the musician. Music is one of the many forms of mediation that make up our cultural substance. It flows easily between peoples, even when language or other cultural practices are dissimilar. The charisma of the musician, like all charisma, is ambivalent. It can simply be technical skill. Or, the musician can use the medium, music, with all of its specific conventions and norms, to thwart the way we are tempted to view her humanity and so prompt us to view anew her humanity as that which exceeds representation. The non- or quasi-representational status of music is in some ways particularly conducive to this sort of charismatic performance because the musician's charisma is so closely identified with the medium in which she performs: she is a charismatic *musician* rather than a charismatic *person*, and yet it is still clear that a person is playing the music. The dissonance is sharp between human performer and music performed, particularly in an age when we are so used to music replayed, mediated through machines such as the iPod or the car radio. On the other hand, it is tempting to identify the performer with the machine, to see the musician as possessing technical skill that reflects a certain human quality rather than performing the human itself. This is where questions of beauty are essential: the musician (or artist more generally) who produces beautiful work thwarts the attempt to reduce her work to technical skill because the beautiful work, by definition, exceeds what could be expected from technical skill. The beautiful work makes us forget about the social practices and institutions that accompany the work—the art school, the conventions of classical music, the reviews in the highbrow magazines—as the work opens us to approach the world and ourselves in new ways.

Alexie's book opens with the lyrics to a song sung by the Indian rock and roll band whose members are his protagonists: "You know I'm lonely, I'm so lonely / My heart is empty" (1). Here we have on display the emptiness that remains after cultural devastation: utter loneliness. There should be a world of myths and rituals, words and images, dreams and worries, but this world has been taken away. Thomas Builds-the-Fire, the lead singer and songwriter, lives on a reservation where there is nothing to do. The fish, which once sustained his tribe, are gone because the river where they swam was dammed. Fed now mainly by bleak government-supplied foods and convenience store fare, the Spokane Indians in Alexie's depiction have just enough government-issued resources to survive, but certainly not enough to rebuild anything resembling their former culture, if that were even possible. What the Spokane face is much worse than poverty. It is material poverty accompanied by the memory of a rich but irretrievable past, a past reduced to caricature by the dominant culture and so, inevitably, by the Indians themselves. This is utter loneliness: having none of the cultural substance with which to communicate to others in one's own community and overdetermined by the fantasy of the dominant culture. The empty heart in the lyrics might suggest a marker of the human, a heart relieved of cultural sedimentations that obscure its empty truth. But this Indian heart is empty in a different way. It does not even have the cultural resources that are the prerequisite to expressing its humanity as empty.

The collapse of cultural substance also means the collapse of authority: cultural substance carries with it normative force, an imperative to do things in certain ways and not others. What is left is a world without fathers and gods, a world without oughts. "A prayer and a joke often sound alike on the reservation," Alexie writes (101). With no higher authority to which an appeal can be made, to which one can pray, the language of authority sounds worldly and base, a gesture toward something that is so obviously lacking that it can only be taken as humorous. Without authority, with cultural substance gone, there is nothing to give shape to time, to fill it with the rhythms of cultural life. Temporality collapses, as evidenced by a fixture of the Spokane reservation who spends each day telling all who will listen, "The end of the world is near." The end does not come, but its imminence is repeated every day, reminding all on the reservation that there is nothing left to fill the time except repeatedly proclaiming the world's collapse. In the face of such devastation, there were charismatic figures and movements that promised redemption through the Ghost Dance, peyote, cargo cults, and the like. These involved, clearly, authoritarian charisma: one among the devastated would proclaim renewal through a return to tradition, but this was the fantasy of tradition, one or a few components of tradition raised up in isolation from their broader cultural context—and identified with a charismatic leader. In a not so different way, "traditional" chiefs and tribal councils, authorized by the colonizing state, would assume the posture of traditional authority without its substance. Alexie vividly portrays how it is common knowledge on the reservation that such traditional authority is simply a way of advancing self-interest. The democratic charisma of the Indian band at the center of *Reservation Blues* is positioned in direct opposition to the Spokane Tribal Council, who are rightly fearful that their authority—actually achieved through the disbursement of US-government funds rather than through tradition—could be undercut by the band's popularity.

While there is a Tribal Council that nominally governs the community depicted in *Reservation Blues*, implementing a set of formalized laws and distributing resources, there is another community member who wields even more authority, and garners more respect. Big Mom has a mystical aura about her: she is astoundingly tall, she lives on a mountain where few venture, she only occasionally comes down to intervene in the community, but she helps community members and the community as a whole solve problems. Significantly, she is not identified with tradition. The Indian community is ruled by men, as it has been for generations. It is men who once passed down tradition, and it is men who have forgotten tradition. Big Mom is orthogonal to this lineage. She has been on her mountain for many, many years, but she does not dispense the wisdom of the past to the people of the present. Those who travel up her mountain, a distance from the community, do not even receive any specific, substantial information. They are simply in her presence, and it helps. Those who encounter her are able to solve problems that seem intractable. For example, Robert Johnson, the famed bluesman, goes to Big Mom after he sold his soul to the devil.

Alexie leaves opaque much of what happens when someone visits Big Mom, leading the reader to conclude that it is really her charisma, rather than her knowledge or ability, that matters. The one moment in *Reservation Blues* when we see Big Mom solve an actual problem, her technique is quite mundane. At a community festival, there is not enough of the star dish, fry bread, for all to have a piece. Amid heightening frustration from the gathered community, Big Mom uses what she calls an "ancient Indian secret" to make enough for all: she cuts each piece in half. This incident suggests that Big Mom is at once extraordinary and ordinary. She has unquestioned respect in the community, but she gains this respect simply by using a capacity that all humans share. She uses practical wisdom, deploying common sense in the right way at the right time to solve a seemingly irresolvable problem. Of course the problem itself was not so difficult, viewed from the outside, but for those involved, hungry for fry bread and worried that it would not be on offer, common sense was blinded. This is democratic charisma at its best: rather than offering a scheme to improve or transform a community, the encounter with democratic charisma reminds each community member that he or she has within herself the capacity to address the problems that the community faces, if only the situation can be seen without distortion. The ability to consistently see a situation without distortion is treated as charisma, democratic charisma, and it must be exercised by one who is both a member of the community and at a distance from the community—living on top of a mountain, like Big Mom, or raised by Pharaoh, like Moses.

Big Mom remarks on the problematic inertia of community life when she sees Michael White Hawk, presumed to be insane, endlessly pacing the reservation baseball field. When asked what she thinks is wrong with Michael, she responds, "Same thing that's wrong with most people. . . . He's living his life doing the same thing all day long. He's just more obvious about it" (262). Michael is the son of the Tribal Council's leader, the heir apparent to traditional authority—which has been, on the reservation, inextricably mixed with legal-rational authority. Big Mom opposes both types of authority because they are essentially authoritarian: they reinforce the powers that be by repetition, and this repetition is absurd in the context of reservation life. Traditional authority repeats what has come before; legal-rational authority repeats formalized norms. Against the backdrop of a devastated Indian reservation where tradition has been lost and there is little life to regulate, most people do the same thing over and over again, unresponsive to the world or to one another. Charisma always interrupts such repetition, but charisma's interruptions can simply reinforce social hierarchies, can become an exception that confirms the rule. In charismatic American Indian movements, such as those surrounding the Ghost Dance and peyote cults, charisma strengthened social hierarchies by fetishizing certain aspects of tradition and identifying them with a practice sanctioned by a charismatic leader. In contrast, the democratic charisma exemplified by Big Mom interrupts the endless repetition of hierarchized life by displaying unvarnished humanity and calling others to do the same. Repetition obscures humanity, reducing the human to one who does this and that, over and over again, adding up to a human life. While Big Mom does not suggest what, alternatively, the human should be conceived as, she does decisively reject any such reduction— and, most importantly, she poses the question of the human as pressing and essential.

The other figure of democratic charisma who has a central role in *Reservation Blues* is the character whose entrance into the reservation opens the novel: Robert Johnson. This is the real life Robert Johnson, the historical figure credited with inventing the blues. He is a black man from Mississippi who is said to have sold his soul to the devil in order to gain his extraordinary musical gift. Like Big Mom, Robert Johnson is a community outsider. He is not an Indian. But he plays a crucial role in the story. It is his encounter with Thomas Builds-the-Fire that prompts Thomas to begin his Indian rock band, and it is Johnson's guitar that transmits extraordinary musical abilities to Victor, the band's guitarist. As with Big Mom, Alexie offers sparse details about what Johnson himself says or does that

might constitute the substance of his charisma. When we encounter him, he is abject, haunted by the pact that he made
with the devil, trying to escape, to retrieve his soul—to find his
humanity. He will find it among the abject, on the reservation,
at the home of Big Mom. Johnson's music, the blues, is also the
music of the abject. It gains its power by expressing what it
means to be excluded, what it means to be outside of the realm
of representation. This expression is indirect. While lyrics may
convey frustration, it is the combination of lyrics and music that
expresses exclusion and that reminds listeners of the way that
they, too, are excluded. The listener and the performer are human but they are often not treated as human, excluded from
humanity, and the combination of words and sounds expresses
this contradiction. Johnson is a paradigmatic bluesman. As the
great music critic Greil Marcus discerns, in Johnson we find
"the combination of voice, guitar, words, and the mythical authority that comes when an artist confirms his work with his
life" (*Mystery Train*, 31). This is charisma at its purest: not a skill
that has been perfected but rather a way of living and acting
in the world that, taken together, results in a sense of mythical authority. To produce that mythical authority, to express humanity at its fullest, Johnson had to renounce his soul. In other
words, Johnson had to set aside all of the characteristics associated with the man he was, Robert Johnson, in order to show that
the human itself is that which thwarts all our efforts to grasp it,
that which can never be reduced to a list of characteristics.

Having lost his humanity in order to display the human,
Johnson wanders. When he enters the reservation, he states,
"Been lost a while, I suppose" (4). Johnson cannot find a home
in any community because doing so requires a soul. Doing so
would build back up the humanity that he has renounced. He
eventually wanders to the reservation because it is a place where

he can find others whose humanity has been taken away—sold via villainous contract with the devil that is settler colonialism. It might seem as if Johnson, the wanderer, must possess unmediated charisma. Seemingly without family or community, without tradition, if Johnson is charismatic, would it not have to be through a sort of direct presence that would necessarily be authoritarian? Yet there is mediation involved in his charisma, mediation that is so obvious it is easy to overlook. Music is essential to his charisma, and even if he is a musical innovator, or musical genius, his charisma still travels through the repertoire of sounds, performances, and technologies that make up twentieth-century American music. This is what he shares with the Indian band when his guitar passes to them. He reminds them that, despite the cultural devastation around them, not everything is taken away. There are still traditions in which they participate and through which they can express themselves. He and they have lost their souls, but the lonely black man shows the Indians that they still have the potential to embrace what it means to be human. This display of humanity is deeply connected with beauty. Johnson himself, impossible to separate from his music, is first described as not being "ugly," "just marked by loneliness" (4).

There is another form of mediation that persists on the reservation even when the substance of tradition seems to have been lost. Alexie vividly portrays a world of dreams and stories, many of them reported by the protagonist, Thomas. Even though the community does not remember or is not able to perform the social practices of their ancestors, Thomas's dreams and visions provide a unifying medium for the reservation world. These dreams and visions are not of the ancestors long gone; they are of Thomas's world, people he knew, people known to the reservation or through stories familiar to the reservation. Even though most of the Spokane are not interested in such dreams and visions and only grudgingly tolerate Thomas's retellings, Thomas's stories are irresistible. They haunt those who hear them, and they spread like a mist throughout the community. *Reservation Blues* positions itself as part of this mist, a retelling of the retelling, a documentation of the many stories that make up the cultural substance of a community seemingly lacking in any solid culture. The novel's borrowings from the techniques of magical realism prioritize this world of dreams and visions above the positivist world of people and events to which the reader is tempted to gravitate. The charisma that the Indian band displays in *Reservation Blues* brings together the mediation of American music and the mediation of reservation dreams and visions. Those dreams and visions, through Thomas's authorship, are encapsulated in the band's lyrics, brought together with the sounds inflected by Robert Johnson's guitar. The band and particularly its lead singer, Thomas, are charismatic because of their critical engagement with these forms of mediation, their ability to both depend on mediation and highlight the ways that it conceals humanity.

In *Dreamer*, democratic charisma was visible for only a moment, when King and his earthy alter ego become one. Similarly, in *Reservation Blues*, democratic charisma is fleeting. The band does not have it at first: they work on their music, perform rather badly, add new members, lose a member, and finally succeed: they win a battle of the bands in Seattle. After that, their charisma quickly slips away, reaching a nadir in a New York City recording studio when they are auditioning for a record contract. Just as King (standing for mediation) and Chaym Smith (standing for alienation), before they met and after they parted ways, lost their democratic charisma, the band in *Reservation Blues* performed democratic charisma in the short time between when they were a collection of alienated individuals on

the reservation and when a big, white media company considered swallowing up their band. The Robert Johnson character
also poses the question of mediation's dangers in the same way
that the King character poses this question in *Dreamer*. Johnson
sold his soul in order to fully embrace a world of mediation, to
become an extraordinary musician. At its best, his extraordinary performances display the human, but this bargain with
the devil also risks full submersion of Johnson's humanity in
the realm of mediation. Just as King moved to Chicago to escape the overdetermination of his image by his media portrayal
as the Southern charismatic preacher, Johnson wanders to
Washington State, chased by a devil bent on stymieing every
attempt of the musician to be more than his music.

Thomas, the leader of the Indian band at the center of *Reservation Blues*, is introduced in the novel in a way that identifies
him with Robert Johnson. Thomas's skin is described as dark,
almost black. Thomas is also an outlier, something of a wanderer, though his wandering takes place within the boundaries
of the reservation. In his social context, Thomas is abject. He is
picked on and beat up by the other young men of his generation
on the reservation. His passion for storytelling and visioning is
treated as eccentric. Thomas rejects the styles of being-Indian,
and particularly of Indian masculinity, prevalent on the reservation. "Indian women had never paid much attention to
him, because he didn't pretend to be some twentieth-century
warrior, alternating between blind rage and feigned disinterest.
He was neither loud nor aggressive, neither calm nor silent" (4).
If Thomas is charismatic, or if he becomes charismatic, it is not
because he fulfills the desires or expectations of his community.
He must offer something his fellow Indians do not as yet know
they want. And he does: no one has ever heard of an Indian
rock band before.

Indeed, Alexie presents the whole band as lacking in any charismatic potential as conventionally understood (that is, as potential for authoritarian rather than democratic charisma). Victor and Junior, the two musicians with whom Thomas founds the band, are inarticulate and unmotivated. To take but one example, "Victor wanted to say something profound and humorous about eggs but couldn't think of anything, so he farted instead" (74). However, Alexie does present the other band members as well intentioned. At Victor's funeral, Thomas reflects, "He tried to be good. . . . He tried really hard" (281). Victor and Junior do not have natural talents: it is the gift of Robert Johnson's guitar that makes the band extraordinary. They are, however, human. They are not the caricature of Indianness; each has a distinctive and unexpected history of which Alexie only offers glimpses, just enough to remind us that there is more to who they are than what we see in the novel's present. The juxtaposition of Thomas's, Victor's, and Junior's all-too-ordinary lives and the extraordinary music they produce amplifies the band's charisma and assures that it is democratic. The viewer, as well as the reader, is continually reminded that the human is more than it appears, and that the human is not simply culture distilled to its essence.

While in many ways the Indian band seems utterly ordinary, its lead singer, Thomas, does stand out from his community. While most Indians on the reservation are said to acquire their understanding of Indianness from *Dances with Wolves*, Thomas atypically makes an attempt to embrace tradition (though Alexie does not offer much to illustrate what this embrace might look like). Thomas is invested in storytelling, and this is an important form of mediation in reservation life and in the literary text, in *Reservation Blues*. Alexie's description of this storytelling suggests its charismatic significance beyond mediation:

"Thomas Builds-the-Fire's stories climbed into your clothes like sand, gave you itches that could not be scratched" (15). In a context of cultural devastation, Thomas's stories do not offer warmth or reassurance. They do not bring together the community. Rather, they remind each community member of a lack that the stories are incapable of fulfilling. Even before he became a charismatic musician, Thomas was a charismatic storyteller, charismatic in the sense of democratic charisma. His stories had the effect of prompting uncomfortable reflection on the part of those who heard them, giving an itch that could not be scratched, a longing to understand the human that could never be fulfilled. At the same time, these stories, in a context where tradition has been lost, point precisely to this loss and so to the contingency of the stories themselves. Once, everyone was a storyteller; now, there is only Thomas with his odd stories, his stories that do not offer satisfaction. Such stories might prompt nostalgia, but nostalgia has become cliché in this community. The stories are taken as frustrating and limited but also as unavoidable and important. Thomas's community will have much the same reaction to his music.

Thomas starts a band. Their music, from what the reader can tell, is not particularly good, especially at first. They do, however, draw a crowd. They practice in a garage, and many from the reservation stop by to listen. Eventually, word spreads from reservation to reservation that an Indian band exists—not just traditional Indian drummers, but a modern-day, amps and all, rock and roll band. Thomas and his bandmates are invited to perform on another reservation, in Montana. Again, Alexie resists describing their performance as good, or beautiful, or truthful. He does not describe their music as bad either. What he describes is the way that Indians from Washington to Montana are drawn to the band's performances. Alexie is also ambivalent about the cause of this attraction. It could simply be the novelty of an Indian band, or it could be their reputation, or it could just be that they offer an activity where activities are scarce. It is not poor writerly ability that results in Alexie's ambivalence about causation; this ambivalence is quite intentional. There may be many partially explanatory stories that could be told, but what matters simply is that the band attracts a crowd. Resisting a causal explanation emphasizes the democratic, rather than authoritarian, nature of the band's charisma. Causal stories are easy to tell about authoritarian charisma: a leader gives a community what they want, and it is relatively straightforward to describe what they want (power, eloquence, self-affirmation, or whatever it may be). Democratic charisma, in contrast, succeeds in drawing a crowd for reasons that are difficult to put into words. Indeed, this is precisely the essence of democratic charisma: its causal pathways cannot be represented because it displays that which exceeds representation, that which thwarts our attempts to represent. All we can speak of, with certainty, are the effects. Democratic charisma causes viewers to be drawn in and to examine themselves, to reconsider how they see themselves and their world having been reminded, by witnessing charisma, that the way they are accustomed to viewing the world is amiss.

The climactic performance of the Indian band in *Reservation Blues* is the most mysterious of all. The band has been falling apart: two Indian women, sisters, joined from another reservation and one of them has just left. The Spokane Tribal Council is stoking resentment against the band, seeing it as a threat to their "traditional" leadership. Then, out of the blue, the band is invited to perform in Seattle for a huge fee. The remaining band members, with just enough money for gas one way and a loaf of bread, drive to Seattle. As it turns out, they are not to perform for a huge fee but rather in a competition for which the winner will receive a monetary prize. The band's desperation increases as they sleep in their van and then are delayed while sightseeing in downtown Seattle. What happens next, at the competition itself, is quickly passed over by Alexie, but the band returns to the reservation with the prize money—which they split, and then quickly spend. This climactic performance also marks the decisive turning point in the band's history. Where before the band performed for Indian audiences on reservations, now they are performing for a primarily white audience, and their performance becomes mediated in a new way. Immediately after winning the contest, Thomas is on a Seattle radio station talking about the band. After another lull on the reservation, the band is approached by a New York record label, precipitating their ultimate demise.

In a fascinating way, charisma functions as the opposite of alcohol in *Reservation Blues*. As all the characters themselves recognize, the overdetermined image of the Indian is that of the drunk (rock and roll musician is not part of that image in the least). "Most Indians never drink. Nobody notices the sober Indians. On television, the drunk Indians emote. In books, the drunk Indians philosophize" (151). In the novel, not all of the reservation Indians drink, and some of those who drink do so only intermittently. Thomas does not drink, but Victor and Junior do. Alcohol both dramatizes and accelerates the loss of cultural substance on the reservation. It helps in forgetting the past, from last night to last generation to the generations before. It also individualizes the community, causing quarrels and straining family ties. Alcohol marks hopelessness and reminds those stepping over or around intoxicated bodies of the depths of hopelessness. In the novel, alcohol consumption is often closely linked with the breakdown in familial lineage, for example, the death of a son results in a father who had always

sworn off alcohol now allowing it to ruin his life, and a son begins drinking when his father and then stepfather leave him.
Alcohol alters personality, but it ultimately repulses rather than
attracts. It leads to a living death, to a life where nothing happens, over and over—exactly life on the reservation.

Thomas's mother died when he was young, and his father is
always drunk, incapable of playing a fatherly role. Indeed, when
his father first appears in the novel, passed out from alcohol,
there is confusion as to his identity. When Thomas recognizes
his father, he exclaims, "I hate this. I hate my father" (114). Here
the father, incapacitated by alcohol, stands for the substance of
Indian culture as a whole. It is there, in a way, but it is impotent. It cannot reproduce itself, and yet it is not dead. Thomas's
hatred, stated rather than felt, his words seemingly emotionless,
marks a commitment to be different from that which surrounds
him. Tradition and lineage have collapsed into an impotent
stupor, but Thomas realizes that he has not collapsed. He tells
stories, he knows music—as his name suggests, he builds-the-fire.
He does not do so through claiming a manhood that his father
could not fulfill; Thomas was never a lady's man. Rather, in a
world of ugliness, he can create something beautiful. The beautiful stands to the side of procreation and the hierarchies tradition enforces. The beautiful, specifically beautiful music, offers
novelty without reproduction, detached from histories of father-
to-son, parent-to-child transmission. The sounds of beautiful
music resonate with individuals who hear it regardless of biological relation or capacity to respond with a performance that
echoes the original.

Indeed, when Thomas is asked about the origins of the band,
he complicates genealogical transmission. He could have done
this by mentioning Robert Johnson, the black man who in-
spires Indians to start a band, but this would have framed John-

son as too much of a father figure. Rather, Thomas begins by saying "I heard voices" (213). It is out of the dreams and visions
swirling through the reservation, catalyzed by Thomas himself,
that the inspiration for the band came—or so it seems at first.
Then, Thomas qualifies, "I guess I heard voices. I mean, I'm sort
of a liar, enit? I like attention. I want strangers to love me. I
don't even know why." Here Thomas links exterior and interior,
that which transcends the world with self-transcendence. He
represents the confusion between hearing voices, otherworldly
spirits that inspire, that gift a human, and the desire to be loved,
that is, to be recognized for who he truly is. This mixture of
exterior and interior is unstable, and this makes Thomas cau-
tious, describing himself as "a liar," ultimately claiming ignorance. What he does know, though, is that the band, and the
charisma on display in the band, did not come from his father,
and it did not come from his father's father and the generations
before.

The fathers of Thomas's bandmates, Victor and Junior, are
also out of the picture. Junior's father died; Victor's left. Growing
up, Victor and Junior, we are told, acted as each other's father. Before the band formed, they would tease and harass Thomas, but
soon Thomas would enter this mutual fathering relationship as
well. The band at once comprised fathers and sons; the time of
intergenerational transmission collapsed so that now, in the time
of the band's performance, both fathers and sons are present,
generating a new product, music, that would represent reproduction beyond the biological. It would also represent authority
beyond the biological: instead of deferring to fathers or ancestors, those with charisma are taken as authoritative, and if they
have democratic charisma that authority is a deference not to
the powers that be but to the power of criticism, the power to
see the world and the self in terms other than those one is given.

Such alternative forms of authority and transmission are crucial for racialized populations where intergenerational transmission is always already undercut by the authority of the racial majority. Black and Indian fathers are always already second-guessed by the white world surrounding them; to their children, black and Indian fathers are always already, in a way, drunk or absent. When Junior went away to Oregon for college, his white girlfriend became pregnant, but she aborted the child because she did not want to raise a child with an Indian father. Despite his performance of Indian masculinity that contrasts sharply with Thomas's refusal of such masculinity, the white world still attacks the possibility that Junior would become a father.

As the band takes off, two white women start attending their performances. Junior and Victor are excited about the chance to express their manliness with these women. They do, eventually, sleep with the white women, Betty and Veronica, but not until after the women display their racial and cultural domination by spending a night with the two Indians but refusing to have sex with them. The band may have potential for democratic charisma, and at moments this potential may be realized, but most of the time, from the perspective of the white world, the Indian band was no more than a cultural stereotype, used to fulfill preexisting desires but not allowed to leave its careful circumscription. Junior and Victor will fulfill the desires of Betty and Veronica when the women want, how they want. In contrast, Thomas, whose charisma is more consistently democratic, does find a sexual potency, which before had eluded him. It is more than sexual potency: he finds love.

Thomas is drawn to a beautiful Montana Indian, Chess, and he has the band perform a song for her. She is flattered, and love develops. Again, Alexie is often hazy on what this relationship really entails, about what the causes are for this love.

He just shows the effects: Thomas and Chess grow closer to each other. Chess returns to Washington State with the band and with her sister, Checkers. In contrast to the one-sided relationships between the white women and Thomas's bandmates, Alexie describes the relationship between Thomas and Chess as deeply reciprocal: "She kissed him like he was a warrior; she kissed him like she was a warrior" (68). It is not a performance of masculinity that attracts Chess and ultimately restores Thomas's potency; it is a charismatic performance. It is a performance that puts his humanity on display, and it is a performance that solicits the humanity of others. Chess, too, becomes a warrior. She, too, is virile, powerful, and ultimately capable of her own charismatic performance: she joins the band. At the end of the book, once the band dissolves, the relationship between Thomas and Chess takes a turn. She wants children. With the democratic charisma of the band at an end, biological reproduction takes the place of the less conventional forms of filiation that are at the center of the novel, and that are associated with democratic charisma.

This unconventional filiation is a hallmark of musical relationships, and it points to an important dimension of democratic charisma. Where authoritarian charisma leverages the figure of the father to construct authority, democratic charisma takes the role of an authority as an opportunity to prompt self-examination through struggle with that authority. Greil Marcus describes the influence of Robert Johnson in these terms: "All of Eric Clapton's love for Johnson's music came to bear not when Clapton sang Johnson's songs, but when, once Johnson's music became part of who Clapton was, Clapton came closest to himself . . . after year's of practice and imitation, Johnson's sound was Clapton's sound: there was no way to separate the two men, nor any need to" (*Mystery Train*, 26). Love is involved,

animating the relationship between the charismatic and her audience. But this love is not uncritical adoration felt in a moment
of ecstasy; it is not fantasy. It is love that is elicited by the charismatic performance but quickly turns inward, onto the self—not
as self-love but as self-examination (or as self-love through self-
examination). The classic father figure, the one at work in authoritarian charisma, is also internalized, but internalized as the
superego. Instead of prompting self-examination, this internalized father figure praises or condemns the self for following the
norms of the father, which is to say, the norms of the culture. The
musical father figure, Johnson from the perspective of Clapton,
does not compel the child to follow the rules of the father, that
is, to sing the songs of the father. If compulsion were at work, the
music produced from such relationships would be second-rate,
derivative. Beautiful music is produced when the father figure
prompts the child to come closer to himself, that is, to explore
who he is beyond what he is told he is and beyond who his father is. It is this struggle of self-examination that entails intergenerational transmission; it has nothing to do with biology.
On Marcus's account, at the end of the process "there was no
way to separate the two men." This could imply that the musical
son became just like the father. To the contrary, if we are to
take Robert Johnson as exemplifying democratic charisma, it is
not particular qualities of Johnson that are similar to particular
qualities that develop in Clapton. Rather, it is their ipseity that
resonates: what they have in common is that, in the combination of their music and their person, they call into question how
the world would see them. They display who they are beyond what
they are, in performance. And this performance is contagious.

The contrast between authoritarian and democratic charisma
is dramatized in *Reservation Blues* in the contrast between
Christian charisma and musical charisma, specifically, the mu-

sical charisma of the Indian band. There are two Christian churches on the Spokane reservation depicted in the novel, but it is the Catholic Church that has a particularly important role. Checkers, who joins the band after its Montana show, leaves the band to join the church, where she can sing in the choir. Music plays an important role in the reservation's Catholic Church, with the priest singing prayers in "a beautiful voice" (161). He used to be a secular singer, and his new role is in continuity with his old one: "As a lead singer, as a priest, he could change the shape of the world just by changing the shape of a phrase" (36). Checkers was attracted to the Indian band by the band's democratic charisma, but she was attracted to the Church by the priest's beautiful voice—and his beautiful body. The priest would stand in front of his congregants and speak or sing, and they would respond. He would be their father, and he would fulfill the role of father for Checkers; her own father was constantly drunk. The priest would give her what she wanted, or so she imagined. And, at first, he did. They would talk, he would comfort her, and eventually he would kiss her. But then he had second thoughts. He was too committed to his vocation; or, perhaps, he did not want an Indian child. Just as Betty and Victoria ultimately controlled and manipulated the desires of Junior and Victor, the priest, through his authoritarian charisma, would control and manipulate the desire of Checkers, leaving her brokenhearted, her fantasy crushed.

The novel offers a democratic-charismatic rejoinder, in the form of lyrics sung by the Indian band. One song's chorus is "My God has dark skin" (131). In these words, the band reverses the dynamic of authoritarian charisma in its classic mode, with the charismatic God just as classic as the charismatic father. Authoritarian charisma depends on an alignment between the individual authority of the charismatic and the dominant values of a community. In a white settler-colonial nation, the charisma of God must be the charisma of a white God—at least if this is authoritarian charisma. Imagining God as dark-skinned (the vagueness of "dark skin" creating an alignment between blacks and Indians, like the presence of Johnson) does not simply place authority in the hands of one group instead of another. Rather, it performs a contradiction, bringing together that which is most powerful and that which is powerless, and placing this paradox in a position of authority. In doing so, the wisdom of the world is called into question. That which calls for deference (God) is that to which one need never defer (dark skin), prompting those witnesses to charisma, those listeners to the band, to question whether the way the world portrays itself really makes sense. Self and world must be reevaluated.

The verses of the song push this point even further. The words describe the way that Christianity distorts Indians' view of the world. It tells of how traditional hairstyles are removed to create an appearance of whiteness. The song continues, "My tongue was cut out in the name of Jesus / So I would not speak what's right / My heart was cut out in the name of Jesus / So I would not try to feel / My eyes were cut out in the name of Jesus / So I could not see what's real" (131). Note how, significantly, the things that are right, truly felt, and real are not described. What is described is distortion: Christianity has done violence to Indian people and culture, and this violence has distorted right perception and right valuing. The white priest who looks and sings beautifully, who Checkers loves, represents and participates in this distortion. His authoritarian charisma prevents the Indians to whom he preaches from seeing themselves and their world rightly. The Indian band speaks the truth—or, rather, through their beautiful performance they invite listeners to investigate the truth, to again see what is right, feel rightly, and appreciate what is real.

If the juxtaposition of the Indian band and the Christian priest offers one contrast between authoritarian and democratic charisma, the introduction of a record company that wishes to produce an Indian hit offers another. The record company represents fully mediated charisma, charisma that is no more than a condensation of the preexisting cultural values and their corresponding desires. This culture is no longer Indian, it is American, specifically, white American. Alexie does not hide this at all: the names of the record company executives who recruit the Indian band are the names of generals whose genocide resulted in the Indians' current reservation life. In the world of the record company, beauty is detached from goodness and truth—so it is really not beauty anymore but rather appearance, shine. Sheridan, one of the executives, says of the band, "They don't need to be good. They just need to make money. I don't give a fuck if they're artists" (223). Here it is capital that gives cultural substance its shape, and so it is ultimately money that dictates what will appear as charismatic in the authoritarian sense. Money shapes desires, charisma fulfills desires, so money determines what charisma looks like, or sounds like. Alexie is quite explicit about the link between capitalism and settler colonialism. Whiteness was once propelled by military force, by generals; now it is propelled by economic force, by executives.

The executives seem to make promises, seem to offer money in exchange for Indian goods, talent, but ultimately nothing materializes. There is no record contract for the Indian band. They are flown to New York City and they audition, but they are incapable of charisma—both democratic and authoritarian—in the studio of the music company. Why? Because in this new, hostile territory, in the metropole, mediation so drastically overdetermines the perception of the band, and the band members' perception of themselves. The band had been successful because of its democratic charisma, because it could prompt those in its audience to see something new when they witness the band, and to see themselves differently. There was no possibility for looking anew in the record company's studio. The company was searching for an Indian band that would sell records. All that mattered was whether the band appeared Indian. A band that thwarted the audience's attempt to see them as Indian was the last thing the company was looking for—not that it would even be possible to thwart perception once all of the layers of technology, engineering, marketing, and other forms of mediation packaged the Indian band's music for the white American public.

The record company dropped Thomas and his companions, but they did pick up a different "Indian" band, Betty and Veronica's. The company decided that the two white women, who learned their music from Thomas and his bandmates, could be marketed as part Indian. The white women offered a type of charisma that would appeal to a white audience: authoritarian charisma, charisma that affirms white supremacy. Betty and Veronica sing, "And my hair is blonde / But I'm Indian in my bones / And my skin is white / But I'm Indian in my bones / And it don't matter who you are / You can be Indian in your bones" (295). The desires of white listeners are fulfilled and then some. Fantasy can become reality: anyone can become an Indian. This is authoritarian charisma at its subtlest and most powerful. Hierarchy can not only be maintained; its maintenance can be cast as friendly cultural integration, as multiculturalism. This is what the media want, what capital wants, what white supremacy wants. And this is what democratic charisma, at its best, short-circuits.

CONCLUSION

The Justice of Charisma

The tradition of political philosophy defines justice as giving each her due. Such a definition clearly leaves many open questions. The project for the philosopher is to add precision and systematicity to this definition. How do we determine how much each is due and how it is to be given? A theory seems to be necessary; laws need to be constructed, whether formal laws or social norms or family rules. But there is also another approach to clarifying justice. Emmanuel Levinas, this alternative's most famous representative, urges that ethics is antithetical to law and to theory. Giving someone her due means first rejecting any theory that would allocate resources or good deeds systematically. Any such theory ignores the crucial word *each*, the focus on a specific human being who can never be treated as another. That specific individual cannot be reduced to any category, description, image, or representation. That specific individual exceeds category, description, image, and representation. To do justice is to treat each individual in a way that appreciates her individuality, that refuses reduction. (Levinas is aware that justice must also deal in the realm of social institutions and legal structures; these latter must be continually inflected by the ethical encounter.) What this means does not seem particularly clear. It is tempting to understand justice, on this view, as simply the effect of gazing into the face of the other—which seems far from just. But what is really meant by this account of justice is a grounding faith in our own humanity. If only we can see the human in the other, we will automatically, naturally respond rightly, and act rightly as a collective. It is impossible to say, or picture, or otherwise represent what this response will be. Indeed, its function is primarily aspirational. While we might remember times that we were able to access the human in an other, and we are confident that it led to right response, recalling such experiences does little to advance justice. Indeed, they are often counterproductive because we imagine that it is possible to directly access the human in the other, without mediation, when in fact what is at issue is better or worse perception of the human in the other.

What this account of justice does commend, actionably, is the criticism of all that distorts humanity. This would seem an impossible task if everything—every word, every image, every representation—distorts humanity. However, those layers of representation and mediation that suffuse our world do not all distort equally (this is a point Levinas misses). Moreover, they are not distributed evenly across our world. There are networks of mediation, of languages and visual grammars that reinforce one another, strengthening their hold on us and their distortion of the human in us. Racism, for example, does not simply distort our humanity through the use of the word *black*. It involves rich vocabularies and images woven together and supporting one another. Doing justice in practice, on this account, does not arise from gazing into the eyes of the other; it is carefully interrogating the workings of power that conceal the human in the other. The work of justice is, first and foremost, the criticism of injustice, where injustice is not understood as a particular action or even a particular habit. Injustice is perpetuated when the hold on us of distorting languages and other forms of mediation is strengthened. The struggle against injustice then means analyzing both the texture of our representational world (our ways of talking and seeing) and circulation in that representational world (media technologies); then, it involves using practical wisdom to intervene, collectively, in ways that destabilize calcified forms of representation. It may be impossible to see perfectly the human in the other, but we come closer to seeing the human when the cultural substance that mediates our relationship with the other is relatively fluid. Then, it is easier for the other to surprise us, and it is easier for the other to express herself in ways that display her humanity, whether that expression is in words or images or performances. This is what a more just world would look like: a world where the rigidity of mediations that overdetermine our view of others is loosened.

This might seem far from an account of justice that is concerned with the voices of the most marginalized, that is concerned with racism, sexism, and poverty. But in fact this account of justice is centrally concerned with dehumanization, and with those who are most dehumanized. It appreciates that some forms of representation are much harder, much less flexible than others. The victims of such calcification are precisely the most marginalized. It is most difficult to see the human in those whose otherness comes from their membership in a marginalized group—a racial minority, an indigenous community, or those with disabilities, for example. To do justice does not mean being kind to those who are marginalized. It also does not mean redistributing resources to those who are marginalized. Rather, it means challenging the ways that we, individually and collectively, see the world that perpetuates such marginalization. Any careful analysis of these modes of seeing the world will necessarily probe their histories, their interconnection, the ways that media technologies strengthen their hold, and the ways that they advance the interests of the powers that be (those with the most financial, social, and cultural capital). Any justice-seeking intervention will take this analysis as its starting point, searching for connections to be made or broken, deceptions to be exposed, and technologies to be reappropriated. The struggle for justice necessarily relies on practical wisdom, and that means starting where we are, discerning the points at which we are best able to intervene, and holding ourselves back from interventions that will distract from our justice-seeking strategy.

Charisma, at its best, combines the positive and negative sides of justice, that is, justice as seeing the human and justice as the struggle against injustice, against concealment of the human. At its worst, as authoritarian, charisma perpetuates injustice. Authoritarian charisma encourages those ways of seeing the world that already have a hold on us, strengthening that hold. Authoritarian charisma is parasitic on the network of words, images, and performances that already are in circulation and that reinforce social hierarchies, solidifying the position of the powers that be. It gives us what we want, and our desires can only be articulated in those words, images, and performances in circulation. Mediation constitutes our desire. When that desire is sated, we embrace mediation; we feel at home in our culture. But mediation constitutes our desire imperfectly. We have longings that always go unfulfilled. (The first section of Levinas's *Totality and Infinity* is "Desire for the Invisible.") Those longings mark us as human, and they open us to seeing the human in the other. It is through democratic charisma that we are able to develop these longings. Democratic charisma attracts and holds our attention because it puts the human on display. It calls attention to the limitations of mediation, and this is how the human is put on display: by using mediation against itself and so making clear that there is more at work than mediation. Humans are not reducible to layer of representation on top of layer of representation on top of layer of representation, no matter how much the powers that be would like us to be so reduced. At once democratic charisma invites us to see the human in the other and loosens the hold of cultural mediation on us; at once it advances justice directly and indirectly, through the struggle against injustice. And democratic charisma is contagious, catalyzing movements for justice as the ability to see the human and to challenge the forces of dehumanization is passed from one who has democratic charisma to those who witness democratic charisma—and who are then invited to become charismatic themselves.

As we have seen in the preceding chapters, democratic charisma is often fleeting. The centripetal force of the powers that be sweeps up moments of democratic charisma by representing them, by creating and calcifying modes of seeing them that quickly become inescapable. Martin Luther King, Jr., struggled to be more than his media image. The Indian band depicted by Sherman Alexie fell apart when a New York record company showed interest in their music. And Harper Lee withdrew to her Alabama house with her black maid after the runaway success of her novel. That democratic charisma is so ephemeral tempts us to dismiss it, to see charisma as hopelessly perpetuating the status quo, as hopelessly perpetuating injustice. But the best parts of the world are wrapped in equivocation. Truth, goodness, and beauty make for a just world, but they do not travel in the open. They are unveiled through democratic charisma, but democratic charisma is subtle and fleeting. We can, however, open ourselves to democratic charisma. We can learn to discern authoritarian charisma, with its investment in hierarchy, its entanglement in law and tradition, securing the interests of the powers that be. We can stop looking for charisma in fathers, thundering voices, and law courts. We can listen for the charisma of our neighbor, our great-aunt, or our colleague. As we do, we are listening for the call of justice.

There was yet another March on Washington on December 13, 2014. Like many rallies before, it was American racism that brought thousands to the National Mall. This time, it was police violence, made vivid by the deaths of Eric Garner in New York and Michael Brown in Ferguson. The lie had been given to America as a postracial nation with these violent deaths of black men at the hands of those agents of the state sworn to serve and protect. There was racial injustice in America, and the black leadership class knew how to respond. Rev. Al Sharpton's National Action Network called a march. The charismatic Baptist preacher thundered and gesticulated, naming the race problem facing the nation and referring to his own difficult role as a black father. Something was different this time, however. There was a glitch in the choreography. Young black activists from Ferguson grabbed the microphone, demanding a chance to make their voices heard. They were particularly irked that the National Action Network had designated a VIP area near the speaker's podium, a mark of hierarchy antithetical to the values of grassroots organizing. Sharpton's staff quickly cut off the microphone and removed the Ferguson protesters, preserving the podium for Sharpton's charisma alone, and for those he designated.

Critics of charisma, and much of the American left, saw this moment as crystallizing the tension between charismatic, top-down leadership and bottom-up, grassroots organizing. It was Martin Luther King, Jr., vs. Ella Baker. The traditional black leadership was represented by the patriarchal male with the loud voice, doing his best to package and ultimately control the Black Lives Matter movement, a movement led by youth, particularly female, particularly queer. Sharpton might have the ear of the president, but it appeared that he did not have the ear of what was supposed to be his principle constituency: ordinary, justice-seeking blacks. Sharpton's charisma, had it succeeded, would have made us forget about those Ferguson young people as we were lulled by Sharpton's lofty ideals and felicitous phrases, his apparent ability to speak directly to us.

The Ferguson protesters short-circuited Sharpton's charisma, revealing its artificiality with their authenticity. They did not offer an alternative performance—the microphone was shut off too quickly for that—but their interruption was circulated widely on mainstream and social media. Is this democratic charisma, ever so fleeting, not so much a performance as an interruption, calling attention to Sharpton's stagecraft and inviting questions about the political efficacy of his leadership? Such a narrative misses a crucial fact about what happened that cold December day. The Ferguson protester who interrupted Sharpton was not one of the anonymous masses who had spontaneously arisen after Michael Brown's death. She was Johnetta Elzie, Twitter celebrity, followed on that social media platform by more than seventy-seven thousand people and described by the *New York Times* as one of the new breed of activists who leverage "the personal connection that a charismatic online persona can make with followers." Elzie is one of a handful of activists who attracted huge amounts of attention on social media because of their proximity to the Ferguson protests, and because of their ability to use the medium of Twitter to amplify their message. DeRay Mckesson, a close friend and collaborator of Elzie, was the most successful of these figures, accumulating more than 240,000 Twitter followers and appearing frequently on national television as a representative of the "grassroots." Mckesson's trademark vest even has its own Twitter account. Mckesson and Elzie crafted a statement, modeled on the Declaration of Independence, attempting to unify black anger, and their Campaign Zero has crafted ten specific policy demands responsive to the wave of protests against racial injustice.

In short, the interruption in December 2014 of Sharpton's charisma actually marked a competition between two types of charisma. There was the charisma of the black male preacher, still following in the model of Martin Luther King, Jr., and there was the charisma of the Twitter personality, utilizing a new medium to advance the same goal of racial justice. This was not ordinary protester versus extraordinary leader. It was a conflict between two types of extraordinary leaders, each gifted in different media. And both fall into the category of authoritarian charisma. In both cases, the medium is concealed; it is as if the charismatic individual speaks directly to the listener or fellow tweeter. The words or tweets give listeners or readers what they want to hear: confirmation that America is a deeply racist nation and that protest is warranted. Indeed, protest is essential to Sharpton, Elzie, and Mckesson. Protest is what activists do; it is their vocation. Elzie and Mckesson's website is "We the Protesters," and they often claim "Protester" as an identity. This suggests the reactive nature of the charisma involved, consolidating and giving words to the anger felt when racial injustice becomes visible—and later formulating policy proposals to mitigate such injustice in the future. Who the charismatic individual is can be reduced to what she is: protesters, first responders to the nation's racial crisis. The human has no role in their charisma, it is surfaces all the way down. Mckesson's charismatic vest and Sharpton's oft-caricatured self-presentation confirm this; the *New York Times* reported on how Elzie chose a purple shade of lipstick to become her trademark.

This should not imply that democratic charisma plays no role in the present generation of black Americans' civil rights movement. As is often the case, authoritarian charisma overshadows democratic charisma as the former is amplified by media. It has become conventional wisdom either that the Black Lives Matter movement is grassroots and leaderless or that its leaders are Twitter personalities such as Elzie and Mckesson. In fact, the movement and hashtag were started quite intentionally a year before the Ferguson protests by three California-based organizers: Alicia Garza, Patrisse Cullors, and Opal Tometi. Garza is a labor organizer who was motivated by the acquittal of George Zimmerman—the neighborhood watch volunteer who killed the sixteen-year-old black boy Trayvon Martin—to work toward changing the conversation about race by advancing a slogan and creating the infrastructure to organize around it. Garza, Cullors, and Tometi used #blacklivesmatter on Twitter, putting it in wide circulation, but they also painted it on banners at marches, used it in countless organizing meetings, and created a Black Lives Matter website that would link those who care about racial justice to organizing efforts in their communities. In other words, the focus of Black Lives Matter, as it was originally conceived, was not protest at all but building power in black communities by turning nascent politicization into structured political organizing. Instead of claiming the identity of the protester, Black Lives Matter sought to cultivate leaders: in their own idiom, to create a leaderful rather than leaderless movement. Garza and her collaborators worked in the American political tradition of Saul Alinsky, using moments of obvious injustice as opportunities to invite fellow citizens to examine the limits of the world's wisdom and to challenge the powers that be. This is a collective enterprise, but it is an enterprise that grows out of a shared identity as human, each of us exceeding the grasp of the world. It is an enterprise that involves performing the human together, contagiously, in the pursuit of justice. This is democratic charisma.

AFTERWORD

Studying Charisma

There are two quite distinct scholarly literatures on charisma, one in social theory and one in theology. These two literatures met at a crucial moment, in 1910, in a confluence that gave rise to the current popular usage of the term. In that year, the German sociologist Max Weber first theorized charisma; he would formalize his account of charisma twelve years later in *Economy and Society* (Berkeley: University of California Press, 1978), still the locus classicus of social theoretic accounts of charisma. Joachim Radkau's biography tracks the development of charisma in Weber's thought and maps it onto Weber's own life story, with a particular emphasis on the psychosexual, in his *Max Weber: A Biography* (Cambridge: Polity, 2009). On Stefan George, who Radkau believes first prompted Weber to theorize charisma, see especially Robert E. Norton, *Secret Germany: Stefan George and His Circle* (Ithaca: Cornell University Press, 2002). Weber understood charisma as a form of political authority, as deference to a ruler because of extraordinary abilities or gifts that the ruler is perceived to possess. Where traditional authority legitimates norms based on a community's history and where legal-rational authority legitimates norms based on impartial application of systematized rules,

Weber suggests that in charismatic authority norms are legiti-
mated by the endorsement of the ruler. As he developed this
theory, Weber drew both on his own studies of ancient Israel and
on contemporaneous Protestant theological studies, particularly
the work of Rudolf Sohm on the early Christian church. In
addition to Radkau's biography, see David Norman Smith,
"Faith, Reason, and Charisma: Rudolf Sohm, Max Weber,
and the Theology of Grace," *Sociological Inquiry* 68, no. 1 (1998):
32–60; and of course Sohm himself: *Kirchenrecht I: Die geschich-
tlichen Grundlagen* (Leipzig: Duncker und Humblot, 1892); for
an abridged translation, see *Outline of Church History* (Boston:
Beacon, 1958). In Weber's wake, the extensive sociological literature on charisma has paid little if any attention to the concept's theological origins, or to ongoing theological discussions
of charisma. Importantly, and not unrelatedly, Weber and his
successors have considered charisma a value-neutral concept,
bracketing questions of charisma's morality.

The level of scholarly interest in charisma has fluctuated over
the years since Weber. In the second half of the twentieth century, political scientists and sociologists noted the rise of charismatic political leaders in the global South, figures such as
Nkrumah in Ghana, Sukarno in Indonesia, Castro in Cuba,
Nasser in Egypt, and Khomeini in Iran. Social scientists such
as Ann Willner (*The Spellbinders: Charismatic Political Leadership* [New Haven: Yale University Press, 1984]) and Arthur
Schweitzer (*The Age of Charisma* [Chicago: Nelson-Hall, 1984])
enumerated the characteristics of this type of charismatic political leader, using case studies and comparisons to show how
such leaders use language, storytelling, and self-presentation to
cultivate an emotional bond with their followers. This, again,
is a value-neutral approach, considering the social and psychological mechanisms through which charisma operates rather

than judging charisma positively or negatively. Two of the most influential social theories of charisma since Weber have been developed by Edward Shils ("Charisma, Order, and Status," *American Sociological Review* 30, no. 2 [1965]: 199–213) and Philip Smith ("Culture and Charisma: Outline of a Theory," *Acta Sociologica* 43, no. 2 [2000]: 101–111.). Shils argues that Weber was excessively focused on the divine origins of charisma, and that the extraordinary gifts of charisma need not have any connection with divinity; they just must be connected with something a society takes as centrally important. By making a connection between herself and core values of a society, a charismatic leader receives deference from that society. While Shils presents himself as value-neutral, his association of charisma with a society's core values opens the door to a connection between charisma and morality. Smith's more recent work argues that charismatic leaders are only effective when their surrounding culture is committed to salvation narratives that the charismatic leader is able to inhabit. Smith dismisses accounts of charisma that overemphasize psychology, instead arguing that charismatic followers see the world in terms of good and evil, and they associate charismatic figures with access to the good. Once again, Smith couches his argument in value-neutral terms, describing a worldview framed around good and evil instead of an actual orientation toward the good, but his presentation opens yet another potential line of connection between charisma and morality.

Theologians have long reflected on charisma because of the term's close relationship to the Holy Spirit. Charisma is associated with divine gift, specifically with gifts of the Holy Spirit. In one sense, Spirit is associated with breath, with the very force of life that animates humans: "The Lord God . . . breathed into his nostrils the breath of life; and man became a living being" (Genesis 2:7). In this broad sense, the gift of the Spirit is simply the gift of life, and charisma evidences that humans are made in the image of God, with the breath of God. The Hebrew Bible also discusses gifts of the Spirit in a more specific sense, extraordinary abilities bestowed on an individual by God. Bezalel and Oholiab are said to be filled "with the Spirit of God, with intelligence, with knowledge, and with all craftsmanship" to make the holy sanctuary (Exodus 35:31); Samson is able to defeat the lion because "the Spirit of the Lord came mightily upon him" (Judges 14:5); and Gideon summons followers as "the Spirit of the Lord came on" him (Judges 6:34). In these and many other examples, extraordinary abilities are conferred by God, and they orient those who witness these divine gifts toward God, or toward the good.

In the New Testament, *charismata* are the gifts of the Spirit enumerated by St. Paul in 1 Corinthians 12, including the abilities to speak in tongues, to heal the sick, and to interpret prophecy. Divine gifts play a central role in allowing the nascent Christian community to persevere despite severe persecution. In addition to its role in biblical theology, charisma is often treated as part of pneumatology, an area of theology that has become increasingly vibrant over the past century with widely influential work by the Catholic Yves Congar (*I Believe in the Holy Spirit* [New York: Seabury, 1983]), the Protestant Jürgen Moltmann (*The Spirit of Life: A Universal Affirmation* [Minneapolis: Fortress, 2001]), and the Orthodox Sergius Bulgakov (*The Comforter* [Grand Rapids, MI: Eerdmans, 2004]), to choose three leading examples. The reflections of Søren Kierkegaard importantly inform theological discussions of charisma, and they offer a way of thinking transcendence without content, transcendence that is arrived at when the self is understood apart from the way the world sees it. See, for example,

"Of the Difference Between a Genius and an Apostle," in *The Present Age* (New York: Harper and Row, 1962), 87–108. Further, the rapid growth of Pentecostalism over the past century has raised interest in charisma from another quarter—although the novelty of this interest should not be overstated given that the Second Great Awakening a century earlier produced a similar interest in, and controversy over, gifts of the Spirit. (See, for example, Harvey Cox, *Fire from Heaven: The Rise of Pentecostal Spirituality and the Reshaping of Religion in the Twenty-First Century* [Reading, MA: Addison-Wesley, 1995]; Paul E. Johnson, *A Shopkeeper's Millennium: Society and Revivals in Rochester, New York, 1815–1837* [New York: Hill and Wang, 1978].) Finally, charisma often plays a role, either explicitly or implicitly, in the theology of preaching (see Mary Catherine Hilkert, *Naming Grace: Preaching and the Sacramental Imagination* [New York: Continuum, 1997]).

For an overview of how the word *charisma* has been used in a variety of contexts, see John Potts, *A History of Charisma* (Houndmills, Basingstoke: Palgrave Macmillan, 2009). For a sense of the word's contemporary usage, see the first result offered by an Amazon.com search for charisma: Olivia Fox Cabane, *The Charisma Myth: How Anyone Can Master the Art and Science of Personal Magnetism* (New York: Portfolio, 2012). There are many more such books, quite a few self-published. Philip Rieff's reflection on the loss of charisma in modernity offers helpful thoughts on the role "inwardness" plays in distinguishing genuine from superficial charisma—what I conceptualize as democratic from authoritarian charisma. See his *Charisma: The Gift of Grace, and How It Has Been Taken Away from Us* (New York: Pantheon, 2007). Other useful reflections on charisma in the modern world include Joseph Bensman and Michael Givant, "Charisma and Modernity: The Use and Abuse

of a Concept," *Social Research* 42, no. 4 (1975): 570–614, and
Charles Lindholm, *Charisma* (Cambridge: Blackwell, 1990).
See also the special issue of *New German Critique* edited by Eva
Horn, *Narrating Charisma*, 38, no. 3 (2011), and the special section of *Soundings: An Interdisciplinary Journal*, edited by Vincent
Lloyd and Dana Lloyd, *The Beauty of Charisma*, 97, no. 3 (2014):
323–392. Nicholas Bromell's essay in the latter begins to think
through what democratic charisma might look like, drawing on
Emerson and the black power movement, but Bromell's emphasis is more on the aesthetic than the moral. Chris Garces
asks whether democratic charisma might be relevant in understanding the "People's Mic" made famous in Occupy Wall Street
protests. See his "People's Mic and Democratic Charisma: Occupy
Wall Street's Frontier Assemblies," *Focaal: Journal of Global and
Historical Anthropology* 66 (2013): 88–102.

Clayborne Carson's article "Martin Luther King, Jr.: Charismatic Leadership in a Mass Struggle," *Journal of American
History* 74, no. 2 (1987): 448–454, raises important questions
about the limitations of historiography that focuses on a charismatic leader. Carson's emphasis on grassroots mobilization has
been picked up, in the historiography of the civil rights movement, most powerfully and influentially by Charles M. Payne
in *I've Got the Light of Freedom: The Organizing Tradition and the
Mississippi Freedom Struggle* (Berkeley: University of California
Press, 1995). Erica R. Edwards's brilliant study of representations of charisma in African American literature takes Carson's
article as a starting point and examines ways that the role of
charismatic leader is contested: *Charisma and the Fictions of
Leadership* (Minneapolis: University of Minnesota Press, 2012).
Cedric Robinson opened this line of inquiry with his exploration
of how charisma functions to naturalize political order, and his
call for thinking charisma otherwise, in *The Terms of Order: Politi-*

cal Science and the Myth of Leadership (Albany: State University of New York Press, 1980).

On the charismatic leader as father figure, see Theodor W. Adorno et al., *The Authoritarian Personality* (New York: Harper, 1950). Jacqueline Rose offers an alternative approach to challenging the linkage between charisma, desire, and ideology in her reflections on Marilyn Monroe in *Women in Dark Times* (London: Bloomsbury, 2014). Kathryn Lofton offers a dystopic vision of charisma reduced to ideology and capitalism in *Oprah: The Gospel of an Icon* (Berkeley: University of California Press, 2011). Grant Wacker does a particularly good job demonstrating how the juxtaposition of ordinary and extraordinary is crucial to representations of charisma, not only to charisma itself (the two levels, of course, are inseparable). See his *America's Pastor: Billy Graham and the Shaping of a Nation* (Cambridge: Harvard University Press, 2014). On the manufacture of movie star charisma, see Richard Dyer, *Stars* (London: BFI, 1998). For a case study of the transfer of artistic charisma to the charisma of lineage, to the charisma of the parent from the perspective of child, and its tragic effects, see Matthew Pratt Guterl, *Josephine Baker and the Rainbow Tribe* (Cambridge: Harvard University Press, 2014). Some of the most perceptive recent writing on and deconstruction of charisma have come from various profiles penned by the journalist Taffy Brodesser-Akner (see taffyakner.com).

Saul Alinsky's vision of democratic, grassroots democracy catalyzed by "leaders" is developed in his *Reveille for Radicals* (New York: Vintage, 1969) and *Rules for Radicals: A Practical Primer for Realistic Radicals* (New York: Random House, 1971). His biography is well told by Sanford D. Horwitt in *Let Them Call Me Rebel: Saul Alinsky, His Life and Legacy* (New York: Knopf, 1989), and the continuing resonance of his model of leadership is surveyed in *People Power: The Community Organizing*

Tradition of Saul Alinsky, ed. Aaron Schutz and Mike Miller (Nashville: Vanderbilt University Press, 2015). On the fleeting nature of genuine democracy, and I would add democratic charisma, see Sheldon Wolin, *Fugitive Democracy, and Other Essays* (Princeton: Princeton University Press, 2016). On the charisma of the Twitter personalities identified with Black Lives Matter, see Jay Caspian Kang, "'Our Demand Is Simple: Stop Killing Us': How a Group of Black Social Media Activists Built the Nation's First 21st-Century Civil Rights Movement," *New York Times*, May 4, 2015.

Judith Butler offers suggestive comments on representing the human in her discussion of Emmanuel Levinas included in *Precarious Life: The Powers of Mourning and Violence* (London: Verso, 2004), but the discussion of self-reflection and formation in *Giving an Account of Oneself* (New York: Fordham University Press, 2005) has also informed my thinking on these issues. Levinas himself is indispensable, particularly *Totality and Infinity: An Essay on Exteriority* (Pittsburgh: Duquesne University Press, 1969), but see also his *Otherwise Than Being, or, Beyond Essence*, where language becomes central (Pittsburgh: Duquesne University Press, 1998). Although the Jewish Levinas and the Catholic Michel Henry may seem far apart, Henry is also deeply concerned with shedding ideological distortion in order to reveal the human—now as self rather than other. See *I Am the Truth: Toward a Philosophy of Christianity* (Stanford: Stanford University Press, 2003), and, for a more practical intervention, *Barbarism* (London: Continuum, 2012). Alain Badiou's reflections on responsiveness to the (charismatic?) event as constitutive of the human are also most useful: see *Ethics: An Essay on the Understanding of Evil* (London: Verso, 2001) and *Being and Event* (London: Continuum, 2007). I would read Badiou's *Saint Paul: The Foundation of Universalism* (Stanford: Stanford

University Press, 2003) as attempting to offer an account of democratic charisma, but not thinking carefully enough about mediation.

The account of media and mediation developed here has been guided, at a distance, by the work of Bernard Stiegler. See his *Time and Technics* (Stanford: Stanford University Press, 1998); especially relevant is also Stiegler's *Taking Care of Youth and the Generations* (Stanford: Stanford University Press, 2010). Jean-Luc Marion's reflections on the idol and the icon, as developed best in *God Without Being: Hors-Texte* (Chicago: University of Chicago Press, 1991), evocatively point beyond the limits of mediation—toward what I call democratic charisma. Marion locates this "beyond" in an icon, paradigmatically a painting; I would argue that only a person, not an object, can do the work that Marion asks of an icon. Indeed, Marion's more recent writings hint in this direction: see *Negative Certainties* (Chicago: University of Chicago Press, 2015), where Marion develops an account of the human that clearly resonates with the account I develop of the human as performed in democratic charisma. While Louis Althusser does not thematize mediation, in a sense his classic essay on ideology is a move toward mediation, toward recognizing the importance of mediating institutions beyond the state: "Ideology and Ideological State Apparatuses," in *Lenin and Philosophy, and Other Essays* (New York: Monthly Review Press, 1971), 121–176. Herbert Marcuse is a particularly perceptive, though underappreciated, critic of mediation for its role circulating ideology. See, most famously, *One-Dimensional Man* (Boston: Beacon, 1964); see also Siegfried Kracauer, *The Mass Ornament: Weimar Essays* (Cambridge: Harvard University Press, 1995). From a diachronic direction, Alasdair MacIntyre offers the classic philosophical defense of tradition, a key component of what I call mediation, but MacIntyre neglects to consider how media are essential to mediating tradition: *Whose Justice? Which Rationality?* (Notre Dame: University of Notre Dame Press, 1988). See also Jeffrey Stout's development of tradition—again, neglecting media—in his *Democracy and Tradition* (Princeton: Princeton University Press, 2004). Diana Taylor compellingly argues that it is essential to include performance repertoires in any consideration of tradition, moving the focus away from texts and institutions, in *The Archive and the Repertoire: Performing Cultural Memory in the Americas* (Durham: Duke University Press, 2003).

Political theorists have recently begun taking a serious interest in the role of performance, rhetoric, and spectatorship in the context of a democratic polity. This has produced some exceptionally interesting work: Jeffrey E. Green, *The Eyes of the People: Democracy in an Age of Spectatorship* (Oxford: Oxford University Press, 2010); Bryan Garsten, *Saving Persuasion: A Defense of Rhetoric and Judgment* (Cambridge: Harvard University Press, 2009); Jacques Rancière, *The Emancipated Spectator* (London: Verso, 2009); and especially Jean-Claude Monod, *Qu'est-ce qu'un chef en démocratie? Politiques du charisme* (Paris: Seuil, 2012), which also attempts to develop an account of democratic charisma, though with less attention to questions of mediation.

The political implications of Socrates's thought, and the Socratic impulse toward self-reflection and critique, are richly developed by Dana Villa in *Socratic Citizenship* (Princeton: Princeton University Press, 2001). Cornel West also develops the democratic implications of the Socratic throughout his work; see, for example, *Democracy Matters: Winning the Fight Against Imperialism* (New York: Penguin, 2004). Josiah Ober's *Mass and Elite in Democratic Athens: Rhetoric, Ideology, and the Power of the People* (Princeton: Princeton University Press, 1989) offers useful background on the Greek context. The Socratic texts I have found most helpful are the *Symposium, Gorgias, Phaedrus,* and the *Apology.*

On Moses's speech impediment, see Jeffry H. Tigay, "'Heavy of Mouth' and 'Heavy of Tongue': On Moses' Speech Difficulty," *Bulletin of the American Schools of Oriental Research* 231 (1978): 57–67. Michael Walzer's classic account of Moses and the Exodus narrative is found in *Exodus and Revolution* (New York: Basic, 1985). Edward Said's response is found in "Michael Walzer's *Exodus and Revolution*: A Canaanite Reading," *Grand Street* 5, no. 2 (1986): 86–106. Sigmund Freud's iconoclastic reading of Moses grapples with, but also unfortunately tries to answer, the question of his identity: *Moses and Monotheism* (New York: Vintage, 1967). Bible quotations are from the New Revised Standard Version.

Harper Lee's *To Kill a Mockingbird* (Philadelphia: Lippincott, 1960) has attracted a fair amount of scholarly attention, and *Go Set a Watchman* (New York: Harper, 2015) certainly will as well. One recent analysis that addresses both and highlights the interest in a "queer" reading of the texts is Gregory Jay, "Queer Children and Representative Men: Harper Lee, Racial Liberalism, and the Dilemma of *To Kill a Mockingbird*," *American Literary History* 27, no. 3 (2015): 487–522. For a chatty and frustrating journalistic account of Lee's later life, see Marja Mills, *The Mockingbird Next Door: Life with Harper Lee* (New York: Penguin, 2014). John McDowell develops an account of goodness as that which comes naturally when distortions are removed, building on Socrates, in "Virtue and Reason," *Monist* 62, no. 3 (1979): 331–350.

Charles Johnson's *Dreamer: A Novel* (New York: Scribner, 1998) draws on a wide variety of biographical information about King; see especially David J. Garrow, *Bearing the Cross: Martin Luther King, Jr., and the Southern Christian Leadership Conference*

(New York: Morrow, 1986). It is also interesting to compare studies of King's oratory, such as Jonathan Rieder, *The Word of the Lord Is Upon Me: The Righteous Performance of Martin Luther King, Jr.* (Cambridge: Harvard University Press, 2008). Rudolph Byrd is a careful reader of Johnson and reflects extensively on *Dreamer* in *Charles Johnson's Novels: Writing the American Palimpsest* (Bloomington: Indiana University Press, 2005). Nicholas Bromell's reflections on the centrality of dignity to African American political thought put King's democratic potential in a new light: *The Time Is Always Now: Black Thought and the Transformation of US Democracy* (New York: Oxford University Press, 2013). On the overdetermination of black charisma and how to resist that overdetermination, see Nicole R. Fleetwood, *Troubling Vision: Performance, Visuality, and Blackness* (Chicago: University of Chicago Press, 2011).

The characters from Sherman Alexie's *Reservation Blues* (New York: Atlantic Monthly Press, 1995) also appear, with fascinating differences, in his earlier collection of short stories, *The Lone Ranger and Tonto Fistfight in Heaven* (New York: Atlantic Monthly Press, 1993). Alexie's own reflections on these characters are collected in *Conversations with Sherman Alexie*, ed. Nancy J. Peterson (Jackson: University Press of Mississippi, 2009). Greil Marcus's smart discussion of Robert Johnson is found in *Mystery Train: Imagines of America in Rock 'n' Roll Music* (New York: Dutton, 1975). For an alternative account of charisma and beauty, one I would generally associate with authoritarian charisma, see C. Stephen Jaeger, *Enchantment: On Charisma and the Sublime in the Arts of the West* (Philadelphia: University of Pennsylvania Press, 2012). Alexander Nehamas's reflections on beauty are the best recent philosophical work on the topic and significantly influence how I approach it: *Only a Promise of Happiness: The Place of Beauty in a World of Art* (Princeton:

Princeton University Press, 2007); but Elaine Scarry's work is also indispensable: *On Beauty and Being Just* (Princeton: Princeton University Press, 1999). The linkages between settler colonialism and antiblack racism are fruitfully explored in Frank B. Wilderson, III, *Red, White, and Black: Cinema and the Structure of U.S. Antagonisms* (Durham: Duke University Press, 2010). Cultural devastation with particular reference to Indian communities is rigorously explored by Jonathan Lear in *Radical Hope: Ethics in the Face of Cultural Devastation* (Cambridge: Harvard University Press, 2006). It would be remiss not to mention Jodi Melamed's persuasive account of how multicultural literature is so quickly sucked into the racist-capitalist vortex—suggesting just how fleeting literary moments of democratic charisma are: *Represent and Destroy: Rationalizing Violence in the New Racial Capitalism* (Minneapolis: University of Minnesota Press, 2011).

This book may seem rather different from my last two books: *The Problem with Grace: Reconfiguring Political Theology* (Stanford: Stanford University Press, 2011) and *Black Natural Law* (New York: Oxford University Press, 2016). *The Problem with Grace* explores the ways that social norms and social practices mismatch, creating openings for a politics that steps beyond the pragmatic. That book was concerned with the "objective" limits of social norms; this book is concerned with their "subjective" limits, with the way social norms misrepresent who I am. Democratic charisma calls attention to those limits and opens new political possibilities. *Black Natural Law* examines the implications of the account of charisma developed here, taking African American politics as a case study. It shows how four political leaders—Frederick Douglass, Anna Julia Cooper, W. E. B. Du Bois, and Martin Luther King, Jr.—used democratic charisma to call attention to racial injustice and to precipitate social change. These leaders offered public performances of the human that were contagious, catalyzing social movements and critiquing ideology. They reached normative conclusions based on the lack that characterizes the human: they said that laws of slavery and segregation were wrong, that they mismatched higher laws, that is, the laws of an ineffable God in whose image the human is created.

Discussions with Dana Lloyd were particularly useful for me as I thought about charisma, as was feedback from peer reviewers and from audiences at Georgetown University, Wake Forest University, and Brown University. The University of Wisconsin's Institute for Research in the Humanities provided a comfortable environment for writing. One funding source demands more precise acknowledgment: This publication was made possible through the support of a grant from the Beacon Project at Wake Forest University and the Templeton Religion Trust. The opinions expressed in this publication are those of the author and do not necessarily reflect the views of the Beacon Project, Wake Forest University, or the Templeton Religion Trust. Finally, the music of Kimya Dawson, Bishop Allen, and especially Nicole Reynolds has offered me inspiring models of democratic charisma.

INDEX

.

GPSR Authorized Representative: Easy Access System Europe, Mustamäe tee
50, 10621 Tallinn, Estonia, gpsr.requests@easproject.com

www.ingramcontent.com/pod-product-compliance
Lightning Source LLC
Chambersburg PA
CBHW032136020426
42334CB00016B/1187